The Silent Film Quarterly
Volume 1, Issue III
Spring 2016

Second Edition

Edited by Charles Epting

The Silent Film Quarterly

Volume I, Issue 3
Spring 2016

Table of Contents

Editor's Message

Happy New Year from *Silent Film Quarterly*! 2016 is already looking like a great year for the magazine, and there are a lot of exciting things coming up that I cannot wait to share with the readers.

As proud as I was of the first two issues, I honestly believe that Issue 3 is a new high-water mark for *Silent Film Quarterly*. The most exciting moment in the short history of the publication came when I received an email inquiring whether I wanted to interview Carl Davis as part of his 80th birthday celebration this year. As a huge fan of Mr. Davis's work, such an opportunity was nothing short of an honor. I believe that his interview, which kicks off the original content in this issue, is an extremely informative and interesting read, and I hope that other silent film fans enjoy it as much as I enjoyed conducting it.

The other articles in this issue are equally exciting: a longtime friend of mine attended a Chaplin screening in Kurdistan and an article on Jackie Coogan coincides with the new Criterion Collection release of *The Kid*, to name just a couple. There are more feature articles in this issue than either of the first two, and the range of topics is impressive in my mind.

Word has spread like wildfire about *Silent Film Quarterly*, and I there are several people I'd like to thank. Tyler Smith welcomed me on his podcast, *Battleship Pretension*, to discuss all things silent. The episode has received a lot of positive feedback, and hopefully helped to turn some new people on to silent films. Following that, I also was a guest on Jim Rohner's *I Do Movies Badly* podcast, where we had a fantastic chat about the films of Charlie Chaplin.

I also want to thank Rena Kiehn and the folks at the Niles Essanay Silent Film Museum, who continue to stock *Silent Film Quarterly* in the museum's gift shop. Having the support of the only silent film museum in North America means a lot to the publication.

The coming months will be just as busy as the last few have! Already a successful Kickstarter campaign has allowed the reproduction of a 1916 deck of silent film playing cards, and other similar endeavors are currently in the works. It is my hope in the coming months to launch Silent Film Quarterly Press, an arm of the operation dedicated to republishing out-of-print texts from the silent era—autobiographies, histories, you name it. The design of these publications would be consistent with the magazine, and I think they will make a wonderful addition to the bookshelves of silent film buffs.

So without further ado, here is Issue 3 of *Silent Film Quarterly*! I hope you enjoy reading, and as always I hope it does justice to the remarkable men and women of the silent era.

Your editor,
Charles Epting

Write for Silent Film Quarterly!

Want to write for *Silent Film Quarterly*? The magazine is always looking for interesting original content about the silent era, including feature articles and reviews of silent films. Please contact the editor at charleseptingauthor@gmail.com if interested or for more information.

In Their Own Words
Primary sources from the silent era
• • •

Chaplin Not a Bolshevist, Says Man Who Knows Him Intimately
By Mack Sennett
From Detroit Free Press,
October 23, 1921

I have often been asked the question: "Is Charlie Chaplin a bolshevik?" So, by the way, has Chaplin himself been pestered with the identical query. I believe the notion had its foundation in a subscription of $5,000 made by the little man to a socialistic fund organized by Max Eastman, a speaker of a very fiery order, whom the authorities of Los Angeles looked upon with a cold eye.

Since the political opinions of a man who is an artist first, last and all the time seem to be of much interest, it may be as well to say that Chaplin's answer to the direct question was made in my hearing.

"A bolshevik is a man who wants to take away what people have got, isn't he?" Chaplin asked. And, being answered in the affirmative, went on:

"Well, I've worked like a dog for what I've got, and I don't want anybody to take it away from me. I want to keep it; and if there's any giving to be done, I prefer to do it myself."

As I say, Chaplin is as artist all the time, and, like all artists, he has the habit of expressing his varying moods in extreme speech. He had a very hard time as a boy and a young man, and there are occasions when the memory of his former hardships moves strongly within him, and impels him to bitter speech. His sympathies are with the poor and downtrodden; and he has the same hatred of official and legal oppression of the poor which characterized Dickens.

Charlie Chaplin's important associates and friends in filmland, as everybody knows, are Douglas Fairbanks and Mary Pickford. The three are fast friends, and Mary Pickford and her husband have learned to know Chaplin in his eeriest moods, and to fathom all that lies under his spells of strange eccentricity and moody silence.

With intimates such an these, Chaplin's mood turns suddenly from grave to gay; and it is no unusual thing for him and Douglas Fairbanks suddenly to give themselves up to boyish pranks of the most absurd description.

Throughout the period of his unfortunate disagreement with his wife, Chaplin practically lived with Douglas Fairbanks, occupying such apartments of the pleasant house Fairbanks had built for himself as happened to take his fancy at the moment. None of his whims were crossed for one moment, the good friend making a jest of all the vagaries of the little man whom he esteems the greatest genius the film world has yet produced.

There can be no doubt that the unhappiness this episode of Chaplin's career caused him was reflected in his work for the time being. His two most ambitious films, and his two most successful, from the monetary point of view, at any rate, have been "Shoulder Arms" and "The Kid." Sandwiched in between them were three which were only moderate winners, from the point of view of a Chaplin film. They were "Sunny-side," "A Dog's Life," and "A Day Out."

It was commonly supposed that Chaplin, the most severe critic of his own work the world holds, felt more keenly than anybody the doubt whether he was not beginning to mark time, or even to drop back a little in the quality of his work. The five films occupied him three years in the making, and he was satisfied with only the first and last of them.

During the greater part of the time, he seemed to be on the edge of a nervous breakdown; and tried a good many expedients to avoid going over the edge. One or his ideas was a quiet trip to New

York for a month, where he was made much of, and might have been feted a great deal more than he was, if he had not dodged the bouquets, to employ his term.

He came back to the west considerably better, and with a good many dry and caustic stories of his New York experiences. The newspaper men there seemed to expect to find in the man who had risen to fame and wealth in so short a time a Coal-Oil Johnny, who would fling his money about right and left in vulgar extravagance.

"One of them said to me when I was loafing," Chaplin related. "'How much have you spent on Broadway, Charlie?'"

"I said, 'Four weeks, all but a day, and I'm tired of it.'"

"'But how much money?'"

"'I haven't count; but not any that I am missing.'"

"Next day the paper came out with a story that beside me Harry Lauder was a spendthrift. Now I know Harry Lander, and like and respect him beyond most men in his profession. I take it a compliment to be compared to him in any way, and especially for wisdom in the management of my money."

The suggestion that Chaplin is fond of money is, of course, an stupid as it in unjustified. He has always had a supreme contempt for those people who broke into the film business, and presently found themselves earning more money in a week than they had ever heard of. The usual effect has been to make them as extravagant and improvident as could well be imagined.

• • •

The Big Ten and Their Yearly Earnings
From Motion Picture Classic, June, 1926

1. Harold Lloyd...$2,000,000
2. Charlie Chaplin...$1,500,000
3. Doug Fairbanks...$1,200,000
4. Gloria Swanson...$1,000,000
5. Mary Pickford...$1,000,000
6. Norma Talmadge...$1,000,000
7. Tom Mix...$780,000
8. Thomas Meighan...$675,000
9. Lillian Gish...$500,000
10. John Barrymore...$400,000

• • •

A Latter Day Frankenstein
By Eric Von Stroheim
From Nashville Tennessean,
May 21, 1922

I am "The Beast!"

Sometimes I wonder whether to laugh or cry.

The more people hate me, the more money I make—but I often question whether the money's worth it. I think I earn my money harder than any other man; I capitalize public abhorrence.

When I came up the elevator to my suit of hotel rooms a woman recognized me and shrank away. She's only one—it happens every day, a dozen times. That's what I am getting paid for. They call me "the man you love to hate."

I'm just a simple, inoffensive fellow who tries conscientiously to do his best in acting unpleasant parts.

Perhaps it's because I try to do it with subtlety, and don't do it in an artificial manner, that they confuse the part I play with the man I am; however that may be, they do it. I don't mind being hated on the screen, but it's mighty tough to be hated off it: after hours, when one longs for human companionship and gets, instead, unadulterated, Simon-pure hate from practically all with whom one comes in contact.

Here are a few incidents—a few out of so many I can't remember them, but only I feel the sting of their accumulated venom.

One night during a trip to New York I dined at the "L'Aiglon," a popular French restaurant, with my wife and several friends. At the next table sat two couples, and presently one of the girls recognized me. They whispered together for a minute, then one of them demanded, loudly enough for my party to hear: "Do we have to dine at the next table to that beast?" They paid their bills and left their unfinished meal. Of course, we were terribly embarrassed.

One day I was riding in a street car when a woman and small girl boarded it and sat opposite. The little girl looked at me for a moment. "Look, mamma," she observed, "there's that bad man that threw the baby out of the window!" And I love children, too!

A friend of mine was discussing me with a woman friend once, and remarked that I went to her church.

"He goes there," she answered, "but he doesn't belong there!"

They won't even let me go to their churches, and if I didn't go to church they'd lay that up against me, too.

I can take off the uniform, cap, sword, monocle, perfume-behind-the-ears, and other accoutrements of warfare, and be human after the day's work is over. I'm still the beast—not fit to mingle with people or to go to their churches; not fit for the companionship of women or little children —the loneliest man in the world. Why?

Other villains of the screen don't get the same treatment. When my friend Lon Chaney enters a public place, the people look at him with respect. "There's Lon Chaney," they say. "He'a a great actor and wonderful villain. Remember him in 'The Penalty' or 'The Miracle Man'?"

But when I come in they say, "Heres comes Von Stroheim—that beast!"

Even my family suffers from the evil aura that has surrounded me. My brother-in-law, a San Francisco automobile man, was approached by a friend the other day. "I am talking to you as a friend," said this man. "And because of all the gossip. Your sister is the wife of this Von Stroheim. All our friends say he is as bad off the screen as on it. They say he beats his wife and mistreats her shamefully. Now, I know you wouldn't let your sister be married to that

kind of a man—and I want to tell these people, from you. Just what he is."

I was buying an automobile, a birthday gift for my wife, at the time. My brother-in-law introduced us.

But usually there is no brother-in-law present to protect me from the gossip that piles up hate against me. And the more it piles up the more money I'm worth—and the harder it becomes to earn it.

People see the man differently from the actor in other cases—why not in mine? I am just a quiet, inoffensive chap who tries to do his best by his family and do his best by his employer. I play the part of a villain —some one has to—but when I end the day's work on the picture lot the character of the play dies with the whistle that blows "quitting time." People here didn't hate me in the old days in San Francisco and Oakland, or when I was a guide on Tamalpais, when they saw only Von Stroheim, and not the parts he has since played. I was married here and I lived among the people just as anyone else. I am no different now from then.

Still—now they hate me.

Men hate me more than women— perhaps because I am giving away some of the tricks of the trade when I play my villainous roles. Who knows? It's male against male—one male resenting in the other whatever attraction for the opposite sex that the other may seem to exercise. They see the Russian officer in his conquests—and they grit their teeth and rage and forget that he's no real officer and no real villain—but only poor old Erich Von Stroheim, perspiring under Cooper Hewitt lights, to make a living for himself and family.

There was a story once of a man named Frankenstein, who reared a monster that finally rose and destroyed him. I know how he felt. I am Frankenstein of the films —and the monster is beyond my control.

Still—I can't blame the people who hate me—they're my bread and butter!

• • •

Broken-Hearted
By Florence Lawrence
From Billboard,
May 20, 1916

I was hurt, but my back was a-mendin';
    It was shinin' and bright outside;
I longed to be out with spring and the birds,
    And tear up the ground far and wide.

I was hurt, but my nerves were better;
    The doctors bad done a good job;
Improvin', but not fit to work yet,
    But I'm hopin' and prayin' to God.

But it ain't my back nor my nerves, tho,
    That causes me most of the pain;
My heart is just about bustin',
    But I ain't goin' to complain.

I'd like to be out with nature;
    There ain't no heartaches there;
You don't need no doctors nor nurses,
    But just a lot of fresh air.

• • •

Charlie Chaplin Writes
By Charlie Chaplin
From Fall In,
March 25, 1916

In your esteemed letter of February 2 you ask if, as a former London man, would I be good enough to send a message to the many London boys in khaki who are doing "their bit" in Flanders, Salonica, India and Egypt. It is with great pleasure that I comply.

Every Englishman—whether he be a London man or not, whether he be from Sydney or Montreal, Capetown or Hong Kong—certainly is proud of the pluck and the sheer splendidness with which ALL THE BOYS have and are daily " doing their bit," unflinchingly, without whimper, without stint and without other than the finest of good old BEEF OF ENGLAND spirit. The days of Wellington and Nelson were not lived in vain, for the spirit that underlies present England is no less in courage and in absolute fearlessness.

I am but a player in the films, a good natured bit of a "clown," a popular comedian if you will, a player, but no less a man. I would that I were at the front, as you so strikingly put it, "drilling a squad" with, as you add, "a kick from that wonderful foot of mine." "Wonderful foot" if you will—but with a staunch heart too, if I were there. Those of you there have set the proper pace—I would try to meet it. I am sorry that my professional demands do not permit my presence in the Mother Country; I hope that in so saying I do not sound cold-blooded or hiding behind my player's coat. There are some of us who can not be "at the front," and there are many of you—London men and all—that can be. We cheer you for your spirit, your courage and the cheerful way you are each doing "your little bit." Not only can old LONDON be well proud of her many loyal sons, but all ENGLAND for the men of the hour.

If, in my modest sort of way, in occasional bits of cheery nonsense as "CHARLIE CHAPLIN" of the films, I can instill a moment of brief relief from the brunt of the fray, this is my contribution to the man "at the front," and who may say that it shall not, too, share in "doing a bit" for GOOD OLD ENGLAND, and in helping things and men over the rough spots.

• • •

Box Office Ticker
From Exhibitors Herald and Moving Picture World, February 4, 1928

1. Ben Hur (MGM)
2. The Lost World (First National)
3. No Man's Gold (Fox)
4. The Mysterious Rider (Paramount)
5. Irene (First National)
6. Chip of the Flying U (Universal)
7. Laddie (FBO)
8. The Great K&A Train Robbery (Fox)
9. The Cohens and Kellys (Universal)
10. Rookies (MGM)

Silents in Review:
San Francisco Silent Film Festival's Day of Silents

by Claire Inayat Williams

• • •

• • •

Rather than the usual "Silents in Review department that appears in *Silent Film Quarterly*, this issue features an exclusive review of the San Francisco Silent Film Festival's "Day of Silents." Claire Inayat Williams attended the winter edition of the festival this past December (held at San Francisco's famed Castro Theatre) and provided reviews of the rare films screened.

• • •

For those of us whose great passion in life is silent film and film history, there is something genuinely magical about the lights going down in a movie palace that was built in 1922. The San Francisco Silent Film Festival, the largest silent film festival in the United States, is hosted annually out of Nickelodeon landmark, the Castro Theatre. Once a year is simply not often enough to see these treasures of film the way they were supposed to be seen; on a big screen, in a gorgeous theatre, with live music. December offers a welcome bonus to help tide us devotees over until the main festival, which takes place over the summer. Chinese representation in early cinema, commanding and cunning women, dazzling stunts, and unconventional relationships were explored in the five films at this year's "Day of Silents."

—Claire Inayat Williams

The Black Pirate (1926)

Length: *Nine reels (94 minutes)*
Release date: *March 8, 1926*
Director: *Albert Parker*
Cast: *Douglas Fairbanks as The Black Pirate, Billie Dove as the Princess, Anders Randolf as Pirate leader, and Donald Crisp as McTavish*

Arguably the most iconic role of Douglas Fairbanks' entire career, *The Black Pirate* not only boasts some absolutely staggering stunts, but was also hugely influential in pioneering two-tone Technicolor at a time when it was in serious trouble. Fairbanks, who "could not imagine piracy without color", exclusively possessed both the dedication and the financial resources to see this ambitious project to completion. His enthusiasm for the role is evident in every scene (he was a committed pirate buff since childhood), first as The Duke of Arnoldo and then, following the murder of his father by pirates, as The Black Pirate himself. Swearing retribution, he tricks that same band of miscreants that he is one of them and they capture a vessel, which is carrying the lovely Princess Isobel (Billie Dove). At 43 Fairbanks was still at the top of his game: with sword-fights abounding, walking the plank, swimming under the ship and then climbing up the side of it, sliding down a sail by way of his knife cutting it in half, swinging from the wayward sail to the topsail, and then repeating that whole sequence with the mainsail for good measure. The film culminates in a truly epic and passionate kiss with the Princess (who was in fact his love Mary Pickford in costume with her face hidden), and a fabulous "gotcha" moment worthy of any contemporary action-adventure movie, when the bad guy realizes it is all over for him and the good guys have won out. A celebrated and tremendously successful film, *The Black Pirate* is a quintessential Douglas Fairbanks and one of the more easily accessible films of the day, and certainly for good reason.

Around China With A Movie Camera (2015)

Length: *68 minutes*
Release date: *June 13, 2015*
Produced by: *British Film Institute*
Filmed: *Between 1900 and 1948*

• • •

Primarily a collection of amateur films, *Around China* is an all too scarce glimpse into a country and culture rarely seen in early cinema. It's a treasure trove of history, filmed all over China over the course of half a century by religious missionaries, British honeymooners, soldiers, proud fathers and tourists, compiled (and rescued) by the British Film Institute. What is especially fascinating about this compilation is the distinct Westernization evident with the progression of years. Traditional Changshan, men's formal dress, became replaced with suits, their skullcaps replaced with fedoras; women's dresses became tighter while the sleeves got shorter. Street signs started to include English translations; rickshaw's had to share the road with cars. While the rapidity of the transformation is startling, the most beautiful thing is the similarity to the earliest known Western films, which are simply camera operators filming their friends, family, neighbors, models, dancers, whoever happened to be standing around. In *Around China* we see a group of teenage boys fooling around with a crossbow, street performers; acrobats, jugglers, traditional folk dancers, little girls giggling shyly, ornately dressed Opera singers rehearsing, a newly wed couple

taking in the scenery. I was not expecting to be as captivated with this collection as I was; it turned out to be one of my favorite screenings of the day, we rarely get to see such early footage from foreign countries and its value is immeasurable.

The Grim Game (1919)

Length: *Five reels (71 minutes)*
Release date: *October 12, 1919*
Director: *Irvin Willat*
Cast: *Harry Houdini as Harvey Hanford, Thomas Jefferson as Dudley Cameron, Ann Forrest as Mary Cameron, and Augustus Phillips as Clifton Allison*

• • •

Consider yourself amongst the luckiest of viewers if you have an opportunity to see Harry Houdini in his first ever feature length project, *The Grim Game*. Screened only a handful of times, primarily to other entertainers, the film was lovingly protected and preserved by juggler Larry Weeks for decades before he finally handed it over to

Turner Classic Movies' preservationist Rick Schmidlin in 2014. It's not hard to imagine how exciting it must have been for audiences when the movie was released in 1919 (coincidentally the same year Weeks was born). Houdini was already the stuff of legend, and the inclusion of film into his repertoire offered a much more accessible (and affordable) occasion to see his infamous tricks. In *The Grim Game*, Houdini plays shrewd reporter Harvey Hanford, who conspires, along with his love interest Mary (Ann Forrest) and three covetous business associates, to fake his miserly uncle's death. Their plot quickly deteriorates when the uncle really does turn up murdered, and Harvey must escape police custody while Mary tries to prove his innocence and find the real culprit. We're then treated to many of the stunts that Houdini is famed for; chains, handcuffs, chained to a police officer, hanging upside down from the roof of a building in a straightjacket, and most fantastically, dangling from the end of a long rope over a airplane, from another higher up airplane. Houdini doing what he did best is of course the real thrill here: the slight of hand is so slick you'll hardly notice the rest of the film's shortcomings. Larry Weeks passed away last year, so we can't thank him personally for the salvation of Houdini's inaugural movie. All we can do is help him in his efforts to inspire the next generation of illusionists by continuing to preserve and celebrate Houdini's film legacy.

L'Inhumaine, or, The Inhuman Woman (1924)

Length: *135 minutes*
Release date: *December 12, 1924*
Director: *Marcel L'Herbier*
  Cast: *Georgette Leblanc as Claire Lescot, Jaque Catelain as Einar Norsen, Léonid Walter de Malte as Wladimir Kranine, and Fred Kellerman as Frank Mahler*

· · ·

German Expressionism meets Jacques Tati's *Mon Oncle* in Marcel L'Herbier's *L'Inhumaine*, a film so poorly received at its 1924 Paris premiere that audiences literally ripped up the theatre seats in a riot of disapproval. Our protagonist, Claire Lescot (Georgette Leblanc), is a woman sickened by displays of humanity, only interested in "things she can conquer." She commands a manic, tormented obsession in her suitors, of which there are many, including a young engineer and inventor named Einar Norsen (Jaque Catelain). Leblanc was 51 at the time of release, and had a long and hugely successful singing career behind her. But audiences were not ready to buy into a middle- aged femme fatale, and the enterprising film hurt not only in the box office but Leblanc's own career, who took much of the critical blame for its failure. The surrealism of the film perhaps didn't translate to its initial audience as well…in one prominent scene Claire's dinner guests are waited on and entertained by servants wearing perfectly round and constantly

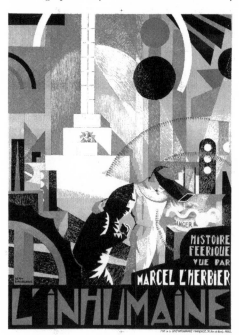

smiling masks, at a dinner table straight out of a Tim Burton movie which is floating on an island in the middle of the room, surrounded by polka dot painted ducks. The film is saturated with creative genius: the sets are Cubist painter Fernand Léger's and architect Robert Mallet-Stevens visions come to life, while Claire is draped in dazzlingly elaborate feathered costumes by fashion designer Paul Poiret. The films' extras included 1920's royalty such as Pablo Picasso, James Joyce, Man Ray, Ezra Pound, Leon Blum, Erik Satie, and even the Prince of Monaco. It seems somewhat unfair that L'Herbier's own name never made it among that Parisian collective, in neither historic nor artistic significance. He certainly was qualified, aside from the content and casting progressive even by today's standards, *L'Inhumaine* experimented with camera movement, framing and light in a remarkably innovative and modern way, all of which make this film truly unique and certainly worth watching.

oudini's film legacy.

Piccadilly (1929)

Length: *109 minutes*
Release date: *June 1, 1929*
Director: *E.A. Dupont*
Cast: *Gilda Gray as Mabel Greenfield, Anna May Wong as Shosho, Jameson Thomas as Valentine Wilmot, and Charles Laughton as a Nightclub Diner*

. . .

E.A. Dupont's remarkable 1929 *Piccadilly* narrowly managed to escape the Hays Code, which was implemented in 1930. Unfortunately, American censors still succeeded in cutting the kiss that would have moved this film up from progressive to revolutionary. *Piccadilly* explored pre-marital sex, women consciously and distinctly using their feminine wiles to gain career traction, and interracial relationships. Anna May Wong gives a vivid performance in what was clearly the part she had been itching to play in her

many years and nearly thirty films of racial typecasting that came before. Sweet and diminutive, but fully aware of her feminine intrigue, Wong's Shosho starts off as a kitchen maid in the dance club whose patrons she will soon captivate. In what is perhaps the most crucial scene in the movie, she brings her English boss and love interest Valentine (Jameson Thomas) to a seedy club in the underbelly of London's Limehouse neighborhood. A black man enters and begins to dance with a white woman, and is subsequently thrown out by the owner. Shosho watches silently, the reality of her situation written plainly on her face. In deliberate defiance of this moment, she presses the key to her apartment into the palm Valentine's hand, with all the stubbornness of a woman painfully aware of her position in life. This action inadvertently seals her fate. A 1929 audience may have agreed to a brief interracial couple but not to a happy ending for them, and Shosho meets a tragic finish. However, the importance of this film lies in Wong's performance; she allows Shosho an intelligence and tenacity unusual for not only a Chinese character but any female protagonist, which is what makes *Piccadilly* such an exciting and notable film.

Silent Film Quarterly *will also be in attendance at the San Francisco Silent Film Festival this coming June 2 through 5. Expect a similar roundup of reviews from that festival as well! For more information about the festival or to purchase tickets, visit:*
<u>www.silentfilm.org</u>

Celluloid Collectibles

Artifacts from and about the silent era

• • •

In 1916, M.J. Moriarty's Movie Souvenir Card Company produced a series of playing cards featuring some of the era's biggest stars. Included were Mabel Normand, Charlie Chaplin, the Talmadge Sisters, and dozens more. The cards were beloved by moviegoers, who were eager to get their hands on any pieces of memorabilia they could that featured their favorite actors and actresses. Movie memorabilia was still in its infancy, and Morarity seemed to strike gold with his product.

Over the next few years, the series of cards would be reissued with varying lineups of actors and actresses. Although initially featuring only 53 movie stars, there are now more than 100 variations known. The cards have proved an enduringly popular collectible amongst silent film buffs, as they capture a unique assemblage of both the legendary and the obscure.

Silent Film Quarterly recently undertook a crowd-funding endeavor to reproduce this set of playing cards for classic film fans today. The project was resoundingly successful; at the time of writing the funding goal was more than tripled.

Although only available for a few short years during the mid-to-late-1910s, it is this publication's hope that the reprinting of these playing cards may solidify their place in the canon of silent film memorabilia.

Reprinted above is an exemplary card from the series, the six of spades depicting "Broncho Billy" Anderson. Below is an image of eight of the cards as they will be reproduced by *Silent Film Quarterly* in the coming months. It is the intention of the magazine to explore opportunities to reproduce other similar items.

The Sounds of Silence:
An Interview With Carl Davis

Carl Davis needs no introduction to most silent film fans. Beginning with his work on Kevin Brownlow and David Gill's monumental television series, *Hollywood: The Pioneers*, Davis played a major role in the "Silent Film Renaissance" of the 1970s and 1980s, and now has over 60 silent film scores to his name.

Carl Davis has had a prestigious career spanning nearly six decades, which has included such highlights as conducting the London Philharmonic Orchestra and a collaboration with Paul McCartney. In anticipation of Davis's 80th birthday this coming October—an event silent film buffs around the world will undoubtedly celebrate—*Silent Film Quarterly* recently had a chance to speak with the legendary composer. Presented here, in its entirety, is our exclusive interview.

• • •

First off, do you mind explaining how you got into the business of scoring silent films?

By accident, not by design. It's very interesting. There was one man who was very central to it, whose name is now Sir Jeremy Isaacs, who was a very inspired producer and did a series in the 1970s called *The World At War*. This was a signature series on World War II, still going around the world, and I was the composer on that series. He then went on to produce a series called *Hollywood* and asked if I would continue with that. This was for a British commercial television company called Thames, as in the river. The inspiration for this series was a book that Kevin Brownlow wrote called *The Parade's Gone By*, and in the 1970's Jeremy gave Kevin, without a budget, the orders just to go out to LA and various other parts of the world to interview those survivors of the silent film period. And he did an amazing series of interviews of the real thing. The people who were there. Because if you think of the early 1970's, there were still many, many significant people still alive and well enough to talk.

So based on that series, I went on from *The World At War* to write the score for the *Hollywood* series, and of course in doing so had to educate myself in this. The journey for me, to use the cliche, was from someone who was interested and intrigued by silent film, as part of film history. During that period, let's say from the 1890's to 1927, there was this significant body of work. I was interested in that, as works of art that were part of cultural history. When it came to the late 1970's when we started to work on it (the series was broadcast globally in 1980), I had to learn a significant amount about the practices of the day, and the breadth of the literature, the variety from low comedy to the highest, almost intellectual levels, historical levels, intellectual levels. It became a very absorbing interest.

So in 1980, Thames Television proudly unveiled this series, and it was a global success. Like a mad fool I said to everybody, "Look, now that I've composed over 300 separate pieces of music, shouldn't we do a whole film, as they did it with live orchestra? With a specially composed score?" Which was the case, I had learned, when it was at its peak. This was the practice. And response was for the British Film Institute to finance a single performance of the huge Abel Gance epic *Napoleon*. So on November 30, 1980, at the Empire Theatre, Leicester Square, in London, I stepped into what I call "dead man's shoes" and actually conducted an orchestra to a new score for a film that lasted nearly five hours.

Why I say "dead man's shoes," is, of course, this way of screening these films was in a sense a lost art. Because once sound came in, more or less from 1927 on, the practice of screening silent films declined and then vanished. Nobody did this. They wrote music for films, but they were recording scores. So the whole question of how do you create a score which you can conduct live and stay synchronized during the film was about to be discovered. Or rediscovered, I should say. And the result of that single performance was: A—more performances because of the outsized success of the event, and B—the same Jeremy Isaacs who had now moved from producer to the head of a television channel, called Channel 4 (named so because there were only at that point three other channels in England), and he said on the basis of the public response and his own response to that single performance, that he would commission from Thames Television a series of silent film classics, restored and with new scores by me, from Kevin Brownlow and his marvelous partner and co-producer David Gill. It's very important to include him. And that's what happened.

The collaboration with Channel 4 lasted until 2000, which is quite

Gance's 'Napoleon', 56 Yrs. Old, Wows London Festival

A still from Abel Gance's *Napoleon*—the first silent feature that Carl Davis scored—as well as the glowing *Variety* headline from the film's 1980 screening in London (where Davis debuted his composition).

extraordinary. Initially, under Jeremy's care, we produced three new films a year, three new restorations and scores a year for seven or eight years. As succeeding managements took over this dwindled to a single film every year, but over the course of a twenty year period, it meant that I had created a repertoire. It was like a walking ballet company, a walking opera company, with this creative repertoire of scores that could be matched to prints. And the reach of it was really quite enormous, and also at the same time building up a clientele of film festivals and orchestras. This climaxed in the late 1970's, with a weekend of four silent films at the Radio City Music Hall. This was in 1977. And from then on, it wasn't like I cracked the States, but there were certainly more frequent performances. The Los Angeles Chamber Music presented them every year, and they still do so. The European film festivals, including those that were specialists in silent films like Pordenone, Italy, wanted the films. It became a feature of every film festival to have one silent film, usually to say, "We have a new print and a new score," and it began to be a cause. So that's the story.

Did you ever expect for silent films to be a major part of your legacy?

One might, as a child, have an ambition to work in film, because it's very exciting. But I don't think, until maybe the last 10 years, that there was a market for writing music for silent films. This was, up to 1980, such a specialty. At the occasional performance you might have somebody playing the organ. Some of the veterans of the silent period were still alive and were doing the occasional performance on organ. They were mostly improvised scores, just on a piano. That's what everybody thought it was, until we, through research, found out it was much more elaborate and meant for a broad public. It was an industry. So we've come back to that. Now there are so many people writing scores for silent films and performing them. There are many people performing films with my scores, and of course it get very confusing about where you get prints and the different companies. It's now very competitive. Even conducting the films is very competitive.

Now it's reached its most absurd period, where normal sound films are having their soundtracks redone so that these scores can be played live. This has proved for the public extremely successful.

My grandchildren just went and saw *Ratatouille* accompanied by the score played in live. I went and saw *Breakfast at Tiffany's*, which was really absurd. There are many problems doing this, mostly having to do with the quality of the original soundtrack, and balancing live orchestra against dialogue. I think there's also a stylistic problem. I kind of resisted myself, and stayed in the main in my repertoire, which has now grown to over 60 films. And I'm continuing to work on it. Because of the new, hugely enlarged broadcasting arena and the industry in DVDs and so on, there is an interest in looking at the films of Keaton, Chaplin, Lloyd, and so on. Those are being very well-reproduced, using the current technology. They're made to look absolutely beautiful. A series of Chaplin shorts, called the Mutuals, made in 1916 and 1917, have come up like roses in the recent restoration by the Cinematheque in Bologna. They look fantastic. Now, from being a curiosity for only specialists, it has really reached a very wide public.

Can you explain your creative process when working on a new project?

I think that the first thing is to recognize that we're not in a situation that the musicians and composers of the silent period were in. Where they were working in a commercial cinema with a turnaround. We're not looking at box office figures. Nor do we have a fixed orchestra. So we are looking at these films, from a musical point of view, as unique works of art. Each one has a character of its own. And so you are able to say, specifically, what's the nature of this film. Does it have a particular setting? For instance, I'm working on a restoration of *Son of the Sheik*, with Valentino, and you have to look at it from the point of view—what's the character of this film? Your starting point is that—what's this film about? Where is it set? What is its character? And your score of course must be there to support these conclusions that you come to about the nature of the particular subject.

So let's say you take the comedies, you might have some idea about what the difference is between an approach to Chaplin or to Keaton or to Lloyd. And of course this is always related to their very unique screen personas. If you think of Chaplin—the background of any Chaplin film is that this guy comes from nowhere and he's always at the door or stands outside of society trying to get in. And so you are there to support the desperation of the Tramp character. There are some rare instances where he doesn't do the Tramp, he had a great success in his early career doing what in England they called the "Drunken Swell." The alcoholic aristocrat, doing drunk acts. But in the main, he was this funny, lost gentleman tramp, always on the brink of survival. You always have to have that feeling, and it's really quite soft-hearted in a way. As opposed to, say, a Harold Lloyd character, who in the main belongs to society. You can imagine a family, though you don't very often see one

in his stories. He is someone who is already a part of society, and in the main he just wants to get on, get further. To be a success. He's living the American dream, from rags to riches. And he has a tremendous optimism, always. Then you have Buster Keaton, who is chronically the dreamer. In a film like *Steamboat Bill*, he takes off on a kind of stream-of-consciousness tack, he'll just go where his interest points him. Once he sets off on what his purpose is, he's unstoppable. The score is there to help him find the locomotive in *The General* or do whatever he needs to do, mostly to get the girl in *Steamboat Bill*, which is, as we all know, this catastrophe. He goes off on fabulous tangents in *Steamboat Bill*.

One of my favorite things is him trying on hats. Normally this would be a question of seconds—he doesn't like the hat, takes it off. But to actually spend nearly five minutes of screen time trying on a sequence of hats, and giving every hat that he tries on a visual comment. Usually just the flick of an eye or something like that,

where you know he doesn't like that one, or he's rather taken with that one. The storm sequence is really like a dream, it's just amazing. I think Keaton is just wonderful. But there's a long way to go. I'll be doing some Keaton shorts, including his very first one he directed called *The High Sign*. That'll be coming up now. But in the mean time I've been in the grip of Rodolfo.

Are there certain genres that are easier or more difficult to compose for?

I would say that the comedies are the hardest to write. They demand a lot of precision, not only in spot events. That's a lesson that Chaplin teaches us in the scores he very closely supervised. I'm thinking of *City Lights* and *Modern Times*. How you have to be very careful not to do everything that's indicated on the screen, and assume some intelligence on the part of the audience. He thought that the disc was so important to the success of the films that you can see in these two films that he makes it very clear what he thinks is the best music for his films. It acts as something of a textbook. I think that the comedies are the hardest to compose but the most fun to conduct. Because of the audience response to them, it's always magic. If an orchestra hears people laughing, they're always turned on by it. They can't believe how much fun it is. From a composing point of view, the broad romantic films are the most fun to write, definitely. And the easiest for me. If you give me a project like *Ben Hur* or the Garbo film *Flesh and the Devil*, for instance, they're highly romantic, so those are most fun for me to write and most suited to my character. So I would say that there are two things—the thrill of writing an effective comedy is just wonderful, but the emotion of the more romantic films is really also just wonderful to do.

Are there any lost films you wish you could score? What about an existing silent you'd like to score?

I'm not too good on the lost films, but I would say because I did so enjoy the Garbo film, there is one Garbo film which is 90% lost. It's called *The Divine Woman*. Quite late in our history, once it was possible to get material out from Eastern Europe, one reel turned up in Moscow, with Russian subtitles. And that is kind of a mixture of *Carmen* and *Tosca*, the one reel is just marvelous. So I wish we could find the rest of *The Divine Woman*. That would be one dream project. Of existing silents, that's harder to tell. I love the Keaton features, and I now have three really important ones. I've scored *The General*, *Our Hospitality*, and I love *Steamboat Bill*. I think other people are doing some of the others, but they are really wonderful, lasting films. So I'd say I'd love to do another full-length Keaton.

What can fans of yours expect in the coming year?

I'm beginning to compose *Son of the Sheik* and have been listening to Algerian music, which is sort of fun. Just to see if I can give it a touch of Africa. I hope TCM lets me do it live eventually, because I've geared it to the size of an orchestra that's possible to get into the Egyptian Theatre. It's a marvelous venue.

Editor's note: In March of 2015, I had the privilege of seeing Mr. Carl Davis conduct his score for Buster Keaton's Steamboat Bill, Jr. *at the TCM Classic Film Festival. The screening, quite obviously, was the highlight of the festival for me. Silent Film Quarterly was still in its embryonic stages at the time, and I could hardly have predicted that less than a year later I would have the opportunity to speak to Mr. Davis about his career.*

I also want to thank Helen and Victoria at Threefold Music for their help in arranging the interview.

For more information, and to purchase Carl Davis's CDs and DVDs, visit:
www.carldaviscollection.com

The Tramp Goes to Syria:
How Chaplin United a War-Torn Community

by Aviva Stein

The Tramp moves cautiously between windows, careful not to break the pane of glass on his back or arouse suspicion of the scam he is running with the Kid. The scamp dashes from place to place, breaking windows with a wind-up any baseball player would be jealous of in preparation of the Tramp's arrival. However, a policeman discovers the con and runs the two out of town, all to a jovial tune and laughing audience.

Rojava, a small region in the north of war-torn Syria, is perhaps the last place in the world one would expect to find a theater of children laughing at the antics of Charlie Chaplin's famous Tramp in The Kid (1921). But in fact, it seems that a little bit of old-fashioned slapstick is just what the doctor ordered. Rojava is a cultural melting pot in the truest sense of the phrase. Although technically still part of Syria, the region is historically Kurdish, and in 2011 when the Syrian Civil War broke out, Rojava seized the moment and declared autonomy. Since then, a bottom-up system of governance has been implemented under the ideology of "stateless democracy," or democratic confederalism. The governing body, calling itself the self-administration, has embraced gender equality, and brought together the area's various cultures, ethnicities, languages, and religions.

It was this ever growing and evolving society which was kind enough to host me for one week, along with a delegation of twenty-seven other Westerners, to experience democratic confederalism in Rojava firsthand, as well as participate in a conference on stateless democracy. While the conference was interesting and the politics fascinating, the true gems of this visit lay in exploring the culture of Rojava and interacting with the people. Each day of our visit, we travelled to various cities within the region. From Serê Kaniyê, a small town on the border with Turkey where we viewed buildings pock-marked by bullet holes and heard stories from families and fighters of the People's Protection Units (YPG)—the main military branch in Rojava—to Qamishli, a town where culture is flourishing against all odds, and the home to the theater where we were lucky enough to join local children and families for the first public screening of *The Kid*.

The Kurds have had a long struggle with culture. Known as the largest nation of people with no state, Kurdish culture has been historically repressed by the regimes of each state they have called home, namely Iraq, Iran, Turkey, and Syria. On November 13, 1960, this cultural repression experienced by the Syrian Kurds manifested itself in a horribly tragic event in the city of Amouda. The Syrian regime forcibly gathered over 500 primary school students for a propaganda film viewing, only for the overcrowded theater to burn down, killing more than 250. However, rather than succumb to the bitterness of oppression and become an intolerant society, Rojava has done just the opposite. In breaking free from the Syrian government, this region has embraced diversity and acceptance from the ground up.

Chaplin, too, survived a long struggle which he refused to let harden him. Growing up impoverished, often sleeping on the streets of London, he found a way to turn his hardship into hope, just as the children of Rojava do every day.

The generosity and welcoming nature of everyone we met was truly a sight to behold, evident even in allowing us to sneak quietly into the back of the theater after arriving for the screening five minutes late. Showing The Kid was not only a way of demonstrating cultural acceptance, it

Children gather in Rojava to watch *The Kid.*

was also a cultural celebration. On November 13th every year, the Amouda cinema fire is remembered and commemorated, but Chaplin's film was the first to be screened publically across multiple cities since 1960. That it was *The Kid* chosen for this honor becomes even more poignant in remembering that Chaplin lost his own first child, Norman Spencer Chaplin, just before pre-production on the film began.

The screening of *The Kid* across Rojavan cinemas was a symbolic reclaiming of culture and power from an oppressive regime, demonstrating that the spirit of Rojava and its people will never be dampened. We viewed the 1971 version of the film, which Chaplin himself scored and edited from the 1921 original. The film's title cards were translated into Kurdish, but all ethnicities were present, from Kurds to Arabs to Assyrians and more. The group responsible for organizing the showing, Komina Film A Rojava (Rojava Film Commune), is a multicultural body dedicated to supporting the cinematic efforts of those within Rojava. Bringing Chaplin and *The Kid* to the Rojavan people is only the beginning for this organization, but it is a promising start for the grass-roots democracy slowly taking root. I can think of no better movie to start this transition towards freedom with than Chaplin's first feature film.

However, this is not to say the screening went off without a hitch. Nearing the end of the movie there was a small scramble to skip a scene where The Tramp dreams that the Kid has died. This brought us back to the reality that all of these children have faced unthinkable traumas in the conflict environment they have been born into. Despite this, there is no denying it was a happy and successful event all around. In a theater filled with laughing children and smiling parents, it was possible, just for a moment, to forget that we were in the middle of one of the most volatile regions in the world. It was also an important reminder that while these children take on many adult responsibilities, they are in fact, just children. Even in a war zone, Charlie Chaplin's language of comedy transcended the toughest barriers to bring laughter and happiness to the audience. The happiness in the theater echoed the high spirits of the Rojavan Revolution, a movement dedicated to fighting for true equality and free expression for all.

While the revolution has only just begun, events like this screening prove that it is possible to bring about change through an inclusive, open system. Film remains an important vehicle for these changes, connecting humans everywhere on a fundamental level, beyond language and experience. Rojava remains a bright light in a sea of darkness, a beacon of hope for the rest of the world. And watching The Kid in that room full of smiles serves as an invaluable reminder that even across an ocean, across the world, across time, we can always find common ground.

Aviva Stein lives in Utrecht, Netherlands, where she studies at Utrecht University.

"A Wonder Child Who is Just a Natural Boy":
The Selling of Child Superstar Jackie Coogan

by Carrie Pomeroy

On February 16, 2016, The Criterion Collection will release a new 4K digital restoration of Charlie Chaplin's legendary 1921 film, *The Kid*. In addition to the new restoration, the Criterion release will feature a number of bonus features relating to the film.

To commemorate the re-release of this classic film, *Silent Film Quarterly* is pleased to present an exclusive article from author Carrie Pomeroy, who is currently writing a book about *The Kid*. In her article, Pomeroy traces the trajectory of Jackie Coogan's career during the silent era, including his unique friendship with Chaplin that was heavily played-up by the media.

• • •

In his heyday, silent star Jackie Coogan was one of Hollywood's biggest draws, lionized as an all-American kid who happened to be a genius—"a wonder child who is just a natural boy," as journalist Thane Wilson put it in 1923.

For Jackie's parents and publicity team, marketing the movies' first child superstar was a surprisingly tricky public relations minefield. The story of how Jackie's publicists, movie theater owners, and journalists "sold" Jackie to 1920s moviegoers offers a glimpse into the challenges of early movie marketing and the evolution of an iconic silent-era star image.

Born on October 26, 1914, Jackie Coogan was famously discovered by Charlie Chaplin at a Los Angeles vaudeville performance in the spring of 1919. Within a few months, Chaplin had started building his feature film *The Kid* around four-year-old Jackie, casting the boy as his Tramp character's adopted son. In real life, Chaplin had recently suffered the death of his firstborn child, a three-day-old boy named Norman, which made the movie's casting and subject matter all the more poignant.

A common theme in Jackie's early press coverage was that Jackie was helping

Image from "Charlie Chaplin's Partner" by Emma-Lindsey Squier from the January, 1921 *Picture-Play.*

to heal Chaplin's grief over his lost son. On September 15, 1919, the *Los Angeles Times'* Grace Kingsley mentioned Jackie in her "Flashes" column, which carried the subheading "Charlie Loves Kid: Finds Comfort in Society of Tiny Jack Coogan."

Kingsley wrote,

> *Ever since the passing of Charlie Chaplin's infant son, it is said he has developed a new fondness for children... There's one little boy in particular who has won Charlie Chaplin's heart—and a year's contract with the world's most famous comedian. The little fellow thus favored is tiny Jack Coogan, four years old.*

The bond between Chaplin and Jackie was genuine and warm. But their relationship was also a boon for publicists, building sympathy for Chaplin and sustaining interest in *The Kid* throughout the film's protracted production schedule.

When *The Kid* finally premiered in early 1921, it earned rapturous reviews and broke box-office records across the United States. Jackie's performance inspired particular amazement. A *New York Times* reviewer wrote,

> *Although the screen's unequaled comedian is in no danger of losing his laurels to anyone, haste must be made to mention a new individual in his company, as much of an individual as Chaplin, and a source of immense delight. This person is a wonderful youngster by the name of Jack Coogan.*

New Republic reviewer Francis Hackett raved, "Without the Coogan boy, it couldn't be done...No child that I have ever seen on the stage created so full a part before..." Charlie Chaplin declared that *The Kid* was "the finest performance of the screen," but added "the credit goes to my costar, Master Jack Coogan."

Rather than trying to repeat the success of his pairing with Jackie, Chaplin released Jackie from his contract in the fall of 1920. Producers Sol and Irving Lesser rushed to sign Jackie and begin production on *Peck's Bad Boy*, a feature based on a popular book series about a mischievous small-town boy.

Ads in movie industry trade publications emphasized the crowds that Jackie would draw in the wake of his success with Chaplin. A First National ad for *Peck's Bad Boy* urged exhibitors, "Grab this one quick! NOW is the psychological moment!" Another ad proclaimed, "Chaplin Found Him—and pronounced him a genius!"

In April 1921, Jackie traveled cross-country by train to New York City to promote the premiere of *Peck's Bad Boy*. During the trip, a new image of Jackie emerged, as an irreverent but sweet-natured boy who had no idea he was a huge star.

The press noted affectionately that Jackie spent much of his journey helping the dining car attendants polish silverware

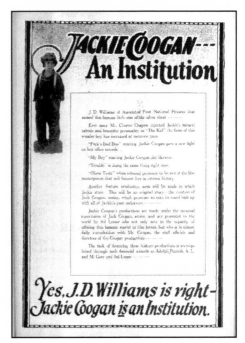

Ad from the June 24, 1922 *Exhibitors Herald*.

and playing cards and dice with them on their breaks. Jackie's willingness to mix with everyone, heedless of race, social status, or income, was depicted overwhelmingly positively. His propensity for playing cards and shooting dice also reinforced his trouble-making persona in *Peck's Bad Boy*, as did his propensity for blurting out whatever popped into his mind. When he met Florenz Ziegfeld, Jackie reportedly took one look at Ziegfeld's striped pants and told the celebrated impresario that he looked just like a circus tent. "Ziegfeld will never wear striped pants again," a reporter noted.

While in New York, Jackie caught a cold after staying up late conducting the Biltmore Hotel orchestra in his *Kid* costume. His illness drew widespread coverage and inspired rumors that Jackie was in danger of contracting pneumonia. A Louisville, Kentucky headline on April 18, 1921 read, "'Kid' in Chaplin Film Battles with Death."

Jackie recovered, but by the summer of 1921, there were signs that the publicity around his New York visit had backfired. The backlash began with a July 1921 *Photoplay* editorial about Jackie. The editor intoned,

> If he were our little boy, he would be learning his little lessons in a quiet home, playing in the sunshine and dirt, eating his bread-and-milk and going to bed at dark. It is quite all right for Jackie to make his pictures...But if Jackie's wonder-talent is to grow into a greater talent by and by it will be because he has what should be the privilege of every little boy who comes into the world—a normal, irresponsible childhood.

Jackie's promotional team got to work crafting a new flurry of publicity to assure the public that Jackie was indeed a normal American boy.

In "Tipperary and The Kid," an article in the June 1921 *Photoplay*, writer

Joan Jordan asked Jackie, "What do you actually think about motion pictures and working in them, Jackie? Would you rather be just like other boys and go to school...?"

Jackie replied, "Say, I am just like other boys. An' I don't see why anybody's got to be so crazy about going to school."

A June 1922 *Photoplay* article, "Jackie Turns Author," was illustrated with photos of a sailor-suited Jackie doing lessons with his tutor. The text was reportedly written by Jackie, complete with cute misspellings.

"I hav a new teacher. I am glad. Her name is miss Newell. She is telling me how to spel what I put down here...What I like to do better than anything else in my whole life is climb."

In a forerunner of today's "Stars: They're Just Like Us" features in gossip magazines, Jackie's "ordinary" home life was highlighted in the May 1923 *Picture-Play* photo spread "Our Boy Millionaire At Home," which asked, "What's the use of making millions if you still have to have your ears washed out every night?" The article featured Jackie's mother Lillian scrubbing Jackie's ears while dressed in a frumpy nightgown. It was atypical attire for a woman more commonly photographed in furs and leaning against a luxury sedan.

At least one commentator saw through the new approach. *Screenland* writer Katherine Albert noted in 1923,

> Jackie Coogan was started out as a child prodigy...but the American public is afraid of geniuses...So Jackie was forced to abandon the intelligent pose and become a regular kid, like any other boy. He must play with hoops and be spanked when he is naughty to make the public love him...

While the press scrutinized Jackie's upbringing and parsed his publicity, movie theater owners were busy finding ways to draw moviegoers to his films.

Jackie's name and image adorned a wide array of merchandise, including dolls, figurines, peanut butter, drink coasters, salted peanuts, and caps. Often, theater owners used that merchandise to promote film showings. For example, Mrs. Emma Shakespeare, a theater owner in Cincinnati, purchased four Jackie Coogan dolls and passed out flyers at local schools announcing a doll giveaway at an upcoming Jackie Coogan matinee, which reportedly attracted a large crowd.

The Strand Theater in Louisville, Kentucky broke records by holding a "Jackie Coogan Ice Cream Party" and running ads urging children, "Ask For The 'Jackie Coogan' Ice Cream Cone. The Kind Jackie Eats in 'Peck's Bad Boy.'" Meanwhile, local ice cream parlors displayed signs advertising the movie, and a newspaper sponsored a contest for readers to submit captions for a picture of Jackie eating an ice cream cone.

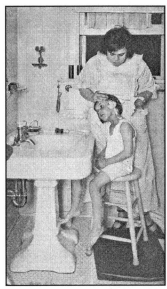

From "Our Millionaire at Home," from the May, 1923 *Picture-Play.*

In Los Angeles, the Kinema Theater held "garment matinees" of Jackie's 1921 film *My Boy*. Admission was one wearable garment to be donated to a poor child.

The *Exhibitors Herald* encouraged other theater owners to imitate the event, urging, "Have your photographer visit the local orphanage and obtain several pictures of some of the children who will receive clothing via the special garment matinee." The writer of the article also recommended getting "some crippled kiddies" in the photos if possible. "These pictures will have little if any difficulty passing the O.K. of the city editors," the article's writer noted.

Jackie's reputation and his movies' rising budgets led to higher rental fees for his October 1922 film *Oliver Twist*. Ads promised theater owners big crowds for the film, but many exhibitors found that earnings did not meet expectations.

Despite these signs of trouble, in early 1923, Metro Pictures signed Jackie with an unprecedented cash bonus of $500,000 and a 60 percent share of profits. Jackie's salary inspired fresh resentment among theater owners. As Hespeler, Ontario theater owner Walter H. Musson put it, "Why in the name of common sense should a person at one end of the game receive such fabulous sums, and the fellow at the other end take a big chance, whether he gets as much back as he pays for the pictures?"

By late 1923, Jackie's image was obviously beginning to wear on many movie fans.

In the November 1923 *Picture-Play*, sixteen year-old reader Emanuel Sharmore praised child actor Ben Alexander, then bashed Jackie.

"Now, will some one kindly tell me why we grabbed at the talented Jackie Coogan, who has only one fine picture, *The Kid*, to his credit and made an idol of him, while we left the more talented Ben Alexander out in the cold?"

An anonymous letter writer from Omaha complained that Jackie was "a clever and talented youngster, but the press agent bunk about his precocity and perfection almost spoils him." Letter writer Louise Comstock commented that she hated to see Jackie acting in movies instead of leading "a natural child's life."

"Hasn't he made enough money for himself and his parents so that they can let up on the little fellow?" she pleaded.

Moviegoer Peggy Mack of Los Angeles sounded another ominous note for Jackie, now nine. She wrote, "Jackie Coogan is reaching the awkward age when it is 'the better part of valor' to retire for a few years."

By 1924, Jackie's image clearly needed burnishing. An opportunity arrived in the form of one of the largest, most publicized charity campaigns a movie star has ever embarked upon.

The plan was for Jackie to helm an appeal for a million-dollar food shipment on behalf of Near East Relief, an organization aiding children victimized by the Greco-Turkish War of 1919-1922. As part of the campaign, Jackie crossed the United States in his private train car, collecting canned goods and clothing, drumming up funds, and attracting crowds and newspaper headlines along the way. It's not clear now if Near East Relief approached the Coogans or vice versa; what's clear is that both Near East Relief and Jackie gained higher profiles as a result of their collaboration.

The Near East Relief Tour culminated with Jackie's arrival in Europe, where he was greeted by thousands of fans in

Store window advertisement for *Long Live the King*, released November, 1923.

England and France. In Geneva, the League of Nations stopped work so staff could witness Jackie being greeted by the secretary-general. In Rome, Jackie had a private audience with Pope Pius XI and visited Benito Mussolini.

Jackie's parents must have hoped that the Near East Relief Tour would be a new start for their son. Instead, it marked the peak of Jackie's fame. Jackie's image as the world's most adorable boy simply wasn't sustainable, and his stardom raised too many uncomfortable questions about child exploitation that his handlers weren't able to resolve. It didn't help that his image as both an average boy *and* a genius was so contradictory, or that his movies had become increasingly formulaic and stale.

By 1938, Jackie was reduced to suing his mother and stepfather for what was left of his childhood earnings, a lawsuit that led to the passage of the Coogan Act, legislation aimed at protecting underage movie actors. Today, many people recognize Jackie for playing Uncle Fester in the 1960s *The Addams Family* sitcom but have no idea that he was once Hollywood's most celebrated child.

In 1972, at age 57, Jackie told *Los Angeles Times* reporter Aljean Harmetz, "I have one claim to fame. The thing I'm proudest of is that I've never been beaten at Scrabble." But then he paused, reflecting.

"No. That's not what I'm proudest of," he admitted. "Everybody's got their pride. No matter what I do now, I was the first. No one can ever take that away from me."

Carrie Pomeroy has published short fiction and essays in a variety of literary journals and anthologies and has published work about silent film in the Twin Cities Daily Planet, *a Minneapolis-based online newspaper. She is currently writing a book for teen readers about the making of Chaplin's* The Kid. *In 2014, she won a grant from the Jerome Foundation to fund a research trip to the Chaplin Archive in Bologna, Italy as part of her work on the book.*

Coming Attraction Slides:
A Guide for Collectors

by Kevin John Charbeneau

Glass "coming attraction" slides are an extremely popular item for silent film fans to collect. Inherently amongst the most fragile pieces of movie memorabilia, these tiny windows into the silent era are much smaller than posters or press books, but can often be just as expensive.

In this article, expert and collector Kevin John Charbeneau outlines the history of such slides, as well as tips for prospective collectors today (Charbeneau is currently working on the definitive book on the topic). He also contributed images of a number of slides from his own personal collection, which accompany the text.

• • •

"Coming attraction" slides are forerunners to the familiar trailers shown in cinemas today, before the start of the feature. In the general term of a slide most people are probably more familiar with the 35mm variety, of the more recent past and today, rather than the slides used to advertise forthcoming feature films, and shorts, during the silent era.

The actual history of the slides themselves is quite storied. Not just something recent, as known, or associated with either the film company Eastman Kodak, or from school lectures. The first slides and projector was invented by a mathematician, inventor, and Jesuit priest named Athanasius Kircher (1601-1680). His invention was called a 'magic lantern,' and projected so-called 'magic shadows.' The first projector and projection of slides happened in 1644 or 1645. Kircher detailed his invention and discoveries in 1646 in his publication *Ars Magna Lucis et Umbrae* ("The Great Art of Light and Shadow").

It was not just Kircher, however—many other thinkers, scientists, and inventors helped to further studies and develop slides and other magic shadow apparatuses over the next 250 years into the development of the film we have today. The projected films of Auguste Lumiere, in 1895, in France, and the subsequent April 23, 1896 presentation at Koster & Bials' Music Hall, in New York City are legendary to this day.

While films of the silent era were projected onto the cinemas' screens for audiences to enjoy, exhibitors needed a way to entice the cinema-goer back into their theaters—the following days and weeks—for the latest films. While advertising with posters, lobby displays, and newspapers helped, these were the days before radio and television. Cinema managers needed another form of advertising to capture their audiences. For this they used a magic lantern slide format which were, aptly called, "coming attraction" slides.

Lantern slides prior to the advent of photography were pictures traced onto glass and hand painted. Later, transfers (similar to decals) were used. When the photographic process was adapted the ability to transfer photos as transparent positives brought a new dimension to the art of projected slides.

These photographic slides consist of two sheets of glass—one that bears the photographic image; the other, is a protective cover over the emulsion of the first. These two sheets of glass were separated by a black paper frame masking. The whole slide was then bound along the four edges by gummed fillets of heavy black paper tape. The slides were generally $3\frac{1}{4}$ inches high by 4 inches wide, although the sizes varied by some countries; for example, in England they measured $3\frac{1}{4}$ inches square. Later slides, circa 1924, consisted of only the emulsion image sheet of glass, which was inserted into a three-fold cardboard masking border/frame. They were larger versions of the standard 35mm slide.

While the films advertised with the coming attraction slides were generally presented in black and white, the slides themselves were usually hand-tinted or painted to add a 'pop' of interest to scenes depicted on the slide. Other information on the slides could include credits (such as producer, director, writer, or story based on, on in some instances stars' names). Along the bottom edge of the slides was a narrow blank border space, known as a "here" area, wherein the manager or projectionist would write in India Ink the scheduled day/date the film would show at the cinema. A companion to the coming attraction slides were trade advertising slides, similar to today's commercials, these were also known as, 'Public Service' slides. Also, song slides, of current day popular songs were projected during the intermission.

Silent films have been seeing new and increasing audiences through film festivals, DVD releases, and film restorations, as well as, recent film releases like *Hugo* and *The Artist*. Yet, with all the new found fascination of silent films, it remains a simple fact that films, especially silents, are vulnerable. It's estimated that 80% of all silent films are lost.

Sometimes, as I've found out through research, these slides are the only instance we have of a particular film's history. As is showcased with the illustrations in this article, even these slides are painful reminders of the fragility of film, and help make the case for preservation of , not just, silent films but all films as preserving our cultural heritage.

An interesting article in the *Los Angeles Times*, dated August 17, 1928, shows that coming attraction slides were fast being replaced by trailers, and even more so with the advent of talking pictures. Slides— which used to get audiences to settle into their seats and relax—were now getting audiences excited, as exampled "when Conrad Nagel, appeared on the screen in his talking trailer for the present picture

Lights of New York, he received a round of applause." Slides were still used in many cinemas up to and through the 1940s, and in some instances, even the 1950s and 60s. However, the coming attraction slide generally met its overall demise during the early 1930s.

Coming attraction slides were manufactured in mass quantities by numerous companies, as well as, the studios themselves. These slides were the property of the studio producer or distribution company, and rented by individual cinemas, along with posters (one-sheets, two-sheets), including lobby displays. Said items were supposed to be returned after the run of the film ended, to prevent unauthorized use. However, because the slides were glass and fragile, many were often not returned, and either trashed, or stored somewhere in the cinema.

In certain instances, you would see a slide where an enterprising manager or projectionist (of smaller theaters) would scratch off the old title and the latest title release inked in, especially in the case of major stars, with their face pictured on the slide.

• • •

The Brenkert F7 Master Brenograph Lantern

The slides in many cinemas would have been projected onto the screen by the Brenkert F7 Master Brenograph Lantern, (or projector), manufactured by the Brenkert Light Projection Company of Detroit, Michigan.

The projectionist with this projector/ lantern would have been able to project images anywhere on the stage or throughout the cinema auditorium. Any shape, size, color, or focus of animated or stationery images, except motion picture films—the varieties of images limited only by the imagination of the projectionist.

The Master Brenograph had two lantern housings—both upper and lower, which were coupled together in every way;

however, both systems could be operated independently. Only the fader—or iris dissolving shutter—in the upper and lower units was linked in unison.

The F7 model projector consisted of the upper and lower projection lanterns, each with a lamphouse that held 75-ampere vertical feed carbon arc burners; the shutter and effects holder, framing shutters, a mask compartment for screen borders or special masks, effect holder for design plates, animated scenic effects and stationary color frames. Then, the slide carrier—adaptable for 4x5 inch slides, or the standard U.S. size of 3¼ x 4 inches, or an insert for English slides of the 3¼ inch square variety.

Standard slides were those for cinema advertising, such as the coming attraction slide for forthcoming features, or local advertising from merchants in the neighborhood promoting their stores' wares or business services.

Dissolving sets made in themed pairs, measured 5 x 4 inches and were a positive and negative image, with a color filter for the various outlines or shapes produced sophisticated changing scenes, with up to twelves slides to create anything from sunsets, haloes, colored clouds, or other atmospheric effects, again the only limitation being imagination. The Majestic collection produced for the Master Brenograph contained approximately 300 pairs and 120 sets in color, allowing projections of simple geometric patterns to more complex scenes, and illustrations.

Glass design slides consisted of a pane of glass that could distort the image(s) or color effect(s).

Animated scenic effect slides were unique, looking more like a movie film reel canister, with a clockwork mechanical drive. Inside the container was a mica hand-painted sheet chosen from a large number of varied designs.

These were used in the effects holder, and once in place the operation of the switch the mica disk would rotate and the

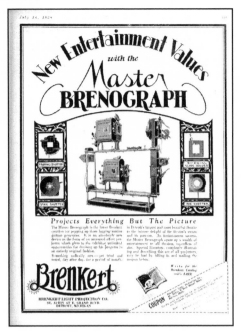

A 1928 magazine advertisement for a Brenograph projector.

image appeared on the screen moving either left to right, up and down, or down and up, even diagonally, at one pre-set speed. Designs on these mica disks consisted of clouds, auroras, falling snow, rain, birds, fish, waterfalls, or shooting stars. Even two separate disks, one as a landscape in daylight, another sunset, when combined with a train panorama slide— the ensuing dissolve effect makes it seem the train is traveling across the countryside during the day into evening.

Panorama slides measured 18x5 inches. Other slides could represent an evening view of the city skyline, with skyscraper windows all lit up, or a photograph of the Louvre museum, in Paris.

Two separate carriers were used for the slides; one operated manually or by clockwork, the other electrically operated. Blending Color Wheel and Gelatin Color Frame Holders. The wheel was, again, clockwork driven, and produced a rippling effect of color on the screen.

Other typical accessories for mastering effects included a Star Shutter or Lobsterscope. The Star was an adjustable diaphragm in a star shape pattern, and could be projected onto curtains or the organ console, producing "charming effects." While the diaphragm of the Lobsterscope had a shape, or effect, similar to an "opening eye."

The Brenkert was primarily a projecting lantern, but was also often used as a spotlight, much like a follow-spot. Depending on the projectionist, the combination of slides and effects, could transform a movie-going audiences' evening entertainment from ordinary to stupendous. I can only imagine how pleased Athanasius Kircher was with the latest modifications of his original magic lantern, circa the 1920s.

· · ·

Coming Attraction Slides as Collectibles

Collectors usually collect a plethora of items pertaining to their likes or favorites. And, when it comes to those who collect movie memorabilia—it's no different than sports fans or toy collectors, to name just a couple. Most collect a favorite star or two (maybe more), or films in a specific genre, or studio. And, of that star or genre or film, it's paper, or books on a shelf about the subject, or posters and photos on a wall, or possible trinkets on a table or shelf. When it comes to collecting coming attraction slides, they are small, but made of glass. Therefore, they are far more delicate to both store and admire. And there no easy way to showcase, unlike framed posters, photos, and autographs, or stacked like books on a shelf.

I began to collect slides, quite by accident, almost twenty-five years ago, having collected just about everything else (books, posters, photos, autographs and most other ephemera). From my first hesitant purchase of nearly seventy-five slides, today the collection has grown to nearly 2,000. They are numerically stored and cataloged, by the slide's number, assigned by me, as I acquire them. They are also entered into a computer database, formatted by me, that I can search and arrange by year, studio, star(s) or other fields of data I have entered. I have the slides stored in files originally used for index cards, not unlike the old card catalog files in libraries. As time permits I add more informational data to the computer as I find it. New cast or crew names, dates of release, or reviews, synopsis information…whatever I can find that might aid in future reference.

Like most collectors, I search high and low, and go to just about any length to acquire new slides. I look online, garage sales, flea markets, word of mouth. Sometimes these are dead ends, and other times gold mines. Sometimes a slide is cheap, but many times nowadays they are expensive, because slides have become a craze amongst certain collectors. When I began my accidental collecting, most people were not interested in the small rectangles of glass, or even silent films, for that matter. They were more an item of the seasoned and experienced collector. Now, more than ever, it's becoming as they used to say in the Twenties, I believe, "All the Rage!"

So, now that you know a little history about the evolution of "Coming Attraction" slides as they pertain to the movies and their exhibition and collecting. Sit back, in your favorite chair, grab some popcorn, maybe a soda, and enjoy a few of the many slides from my collection, and we'll see you soon, "at the 'silent' movies."

Kevin John Charbeneau lives in Los Angeles and is working on what will certainly become the definitive tome on coming attraction slides. On the following pages, images from his personal collection of glass slides are reproduced.

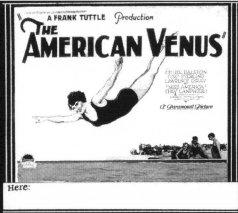

One Minute to Play, FBO, 1926

The American Venus, Paramount, 1926

Ben-Hur, MGM, 1925

Cleopatra, Fox, 1917

Foolish Wives, Universal, 1922

Infatuation, First National, 1925

Lew Tyler's Wives, Preferred, 1926

The Two Brides, Paramount, 1919

The Sheriff, Paramount, 1918

Blood and Sand, Paramount, 1922

The Three Musketeers, United Artists, 1921

Red Hair, Paramount, 1928

The Twisted World of *From Morn to Midnight*: *Examining a Forgotten—and Enigmatic—Piece of German Expressionism*

by Lea Stans

German Expressionism is one of the most celebrated genres of silent film, although many people are only familiar with a couple of the most popular titles to have emerged from Weimar Germany. In this article, blogger Lea Stans takes an in-depth look at one of the period's most obscure and confusing films.

• • •

Silent film fans all know the most iconic films associated with German Expressionism, such as *The Cabinet of Dr. Caligari* and *Nosferatu*. And many are certainly familiar with the more obscure ones, such as *Schatten* and *The Hands of Dr. Orlac*.

But if you go down the rabbit hole of obscure Expressionist work, down past *Genuine* and *Raskolnikov* and even past the lonely *Torgus*, way off in a corner by itself you will find an unearthly drama by the name of *Von morgens bis mitternachts*, or *From Morn to Midnight* (1920).

If you thought *Caligari* was extreme, *From Morn to Midnight* will make you long for the former's comparatively relatable world. Young women's faces morph into skulls. Hand-painted rays stick out from flat painted lamps. Bicyclists glimmer through a distorted haze. This is a film that's exceedingly, insistently, stubbornly avant-garde, a film that's determined to fly over the heads of each and every one of those bourgeois viewers that innocently wander into its theatrical web.

If we're to fully appreciate—or, at least, somewhat comprehend—this film, knowing a bit about the German art scene in the 1910s is essential. The era was a time of industrialization and increased speed in many areas of life, accompanied by a hearty interest in everything new and unique. Expressionism (which had originated in Germany) thrived in this environment, where it seeped its way into art, advertisements, and theater. It took on a layer of angst as artists tried to come to terms with the horror of World War I. Soon the movement was being absorbed by film, resulting in the dramatic set designs and dark themes that are associated with German Expressionism. And at the height of this creative period was born the radical *From Morn to Midnight*.

The plot, if you can tear yourself away from gawking at the imagery long enough to notice, concerns a nameless bank cashier (played by Ernst Deutsch, who later appeared in *The Third Man*) who's grown dissatisfied with his ordinary life. When a wealthy Italian lady (Erna Morena) enters the bank to acquire funds to buy a painting for her son (Hans Heinrich von Twardowski), he's instantly captivated with her. Mistakenly thinking that the feeling is mutual, he decides to embezzle a large sum of money from the bank and run off with her.

He shows up at her hotel room afire with this foolproof plan, but the lady refuses his advances. She also reveals that she has a son—the ultimate deal breaker, apparently. Still itching to escape humdrum routine, the cashier abandons his devoted wife, mother, and daughter and goes on the lam to experience the high life in the city. He buys himself fine clothes and indulges in sports, gambling, drinking, and

ladies of the evening. Inevitably, he comes to the sinking realization that these diversions are even less fulfilling than the ordinary life he had contemptuously left behind.

From Morn to Midnight was a film version of the influential play by Georg Kaiser, an Expressionist playwright with a fondness for Nietzsche. Generally, his plays were concerned with individuals trying to transcend their places in life, and often featured "anti-naturalistic" language complete with long winded speeches. Karlheinz Martin, a stage director known for his daring Expressionist productions, took on the task of adapting Kaiser's play for a young company called Ilag-Film. This was Martin's first foray into filmmaking, and he was obviously determined to make it a memorable one. He teamed up with set designer Robert Neppach, who favored a "jaggedy shapes against black backdrops" look. They apparently put their heads together and decided that if the film

version of From Morn to Midnight couldn't include Kaiser's speeches they would make up for it with über bold set designs. And "über bold" is an understatement.

The designs don't just push the limits of German Expressionism—they shove them. The actors cast noticeable shadows on the crude, deliberately two-dimensional backgrounds. Objects and buildings are stylized to the point of being mere suggestions, with wobbly painted lines serving as architectural details. Every set is a matte black, and every sketchy cardboard door and stick of distorted furniture is streaked and outlined with white paint. The brushstrokes are broad and obvious, as if daring you not to notice them. Even the faces and costumes of the actors are dabbed with paint, making them a part of the decor. The overall effect is as if a blacklight party had gotten a hankering to visit Weimar Germany.

Some notable camera effects add to the already surreal experience. The standout is the "6 day" bicycle race, where the cyclists are stretched with a convex lens and are made to glimmer with the aid of strategically-placed lights. Writer Lotte Eisner described them as being "anamorphosed into shimmering facets." Just why the cyclists look like facets is somewhat unclear, although it could be a reference to a line from Kaiser's play, which reads in one translation as: "I see a circle and a gaudy wavy line." The distortion also gives an illusion of speed, although the cyclists do seem to be pedaling at a moderate pace.

The theme of the film is similar to one that would pop up in 1920s German "street films": the common man attempting to transcend his station in life. Both Lubitsch and Murnau would take their turns adapting it to their own work. Invariably, the dissatisfied main character runs off to experience the thrills of high living but always ends up depressed, despairing, or slinking back home in defeat.

But the theme of *From Morn to Midnight* is less cut-and-dry. The cashier is not only selfish but unlikeable, stealing from his workplace and callously abandoning his family. The world around him is equally cold, quick to use him for selfish gain. The root of all this evil seems to be money, which offers the cashier no escape from an ordinary middle-class existence and certainly offers no easy passage into a life of passion and excitement. And it's entwined in the cashier's hallucinations of young women's faces morphing into skulls.

There could've been even more complexity to this theme if the makers hadn't changed one key element from Kaiser's original play—the subject of the painting the Italian lady tries to buy for her son. In the play, the painting is supposed to be of Adam and Eve in the Garden of Eden. The cashier sees the artwork and connects it with his quest for fulfillment, adding subtle overtones of Paradise and the Fall to the story. In the film, it's merely a modernist painting of a female nude, which the cashier connects with his lust for the Italian lady (who later lies in a posture that mirrors the painting). It's not a drastic change, but it's one with a little less depth.

The ultimate question for this writer is: does all the white paint and flamboyant gesturing work? Is this film a masterpiece of pure, distilled German Expressionism, or is it an overly ambitious experiment drowning in its own self-conscious artiness? I'd argue that it's a bit of both (although I'll admit that side more with the latter).

The film is certainly Expressionist to the core—I've even stumbled across a couple writers who say that it's more technically Expressionist than *Caligari*. The most avant-garde plays in 1910s Germany had similarly dreamlike worlds populated by nameless characters uttering anti-naturalistic dialogue (especially if they had been produced by Karlheinz Martin). You could say that *From Morn to Midnight*, with its complete departure from even a whiff of naturalism, is the most extreme example of a very particular art form.

Still, the film seems strongly self conscious—and I can't ignore the word "pretentious." The acting, while it must've seemed modern in its time, will hardly convert an uninitiated viewer into the glories of the silent era. The intertitles, although faithful to Kaiser's play, are clunky and occasionally disruptive. And there are times the actors nearly disappear into Robert Neppach's most riotous black and white backgrounds. Ernst Deutsch is perhaps the saving grace, throwing himself into his role while pulling off the tricky work of not letting the sets upstage him.

As you might guess, the edginess of *From Morn to Midnight* was its downfall back in 1920. Theater owners took one look at Martin's directorial debut and balked, finding it far too radical for a mainstream audience. As a result it never received a wide release in Germany and never made it to the United States at all (even though Kaiser's original play was fairly popular there in the early Twenties).

In 1922 the film was shown in Japan with some success. And thus, rather fittingly, it's Japan we have to thank for the survival of this oddball work. In 1959 a print was found in the Tokyo National Film Center, and in 1963 the film received its first screening in decades in East Berlin.

Today *From Morn to Midnight* exists online and on hard-to-find DVDs. It's discussed mainly by a fraction of silent avant-garde fans who take it terribly seriously and is largely unknown to anyone else. A slightly dismal fate—but not a hopeless one. It's a film that deserves to be more widely seen, if only because of its considerable novelty factor. It awaits anyone who revels in the bizarre, especially those whose senses of humor will help them glory in its manic, uncompromising visions.

Lea Stans is a film historian who runs the blog Silent-ology. She credits the films of Buster Keaton with sparking her passion for silent cinema. www.silentology.wordpress.com

Tom Tyler:
Silent Film Hercules
by Mary Haberstroh

Tom Tyler had a lengthy Hollywood career, spanning from the silent era to countless westerns in the 1930s and 40s. In this article, film historian and Tyler fan Mary Haberstroh details the actor's early film career, as well as his impressive athletic career off the silver screen.

• • •

Being a natural-born athlete as well as a silent film actor had its rewards for Tom Tyler, and as a weightlifting champion, enabled him to showcase his physical strength talents during his silent film career. He worked under contract with FBO (Film Booking Offices) Pictures from 1925 to 1929, making a total of twenty-nine movies for the film studio. It was also in 1925 when Tom joined the Los Angeles Athletic Club (LAAC), spending his spare time in the gym honing his already muscular physique—he stood 6'2" tall, 190 lbs.—to perfection. By the time he spent a few months pumping iron, Tom was ready to perform any stunts required of him in the film scripts, and at the same time prepared himself for the annual weightlifting competition hosted by the LAAC.

Tom's physical measurements at the height of his weightlifting career from 1925 to 1928 were as follows: chest (unexpanded) 45", waist 32", hips 41". He also gained seven pounds of muscle for a total of 197 pounds in weight. Tom's physique was impressive and of course idealized among the many young boys who patronized the

Tom Tyler in his second feature, *The Wyoming Wildcat* (1925).

Saturday matinee. Along with his handsome dark looks, Tom Tyler was a living Adonis, while his introverted personality made him not only appealing to those he worked with but also his fans. He was ready for his first heavyweight weightlifting competition in 1925, and by 1928, won every annual AAU (Amateur Athletic Union) Southern California heavyweight weightlifting championship. In 1927, he clean and jerked 300 lbs., becoming the first weightlifter in the nation to do so. The clean and jerk method of weightlifting, a lift that Tom excelled at, requires the individual to lift the barbell from the floor in one continuous motion across the clavicles then thrusting it straight above the head into the air. Tom's weightlifting achievements earned him attention in a 1926 issue of *American Athlete*, modeling assignments for Milo Barbells, and ultimately a place on the American Olympic weightlifting team for the 1928 Olympics, held in Amsterdam that year. His lifts in the Olympic competition were as follows: 230 pounds military press, 230 pounds in the snatch lift, and 300 pounds for the clean and jerk method. Even thought the United States never sent a weightlifting team to Amsterdam that year, that was still a significant achievement for Tom Tyler to include on his resume.

Tom's first stunt job on film was as a chariot driver in *Ben Hur* (1925) which was a minor role but provided him with some direction as to where his acting niche would be. He ended up in B-westerns, many which contained common story lines found across other B-westerns produced by other studios in Hollywood but garnished with his feats of strength, modest charm and his engaging smile. What red-blooded American boy would not want to spend his Saturday afternoons at the matinee watching Tom Tyler performing enviable stunts that requires serious muscular strength, rescue the damsel in distress, and smile all the way through? It was these qualities Tyler possessed—and more—that

made him so popular at FBO and with his public.

While most of Tom's FBO silent films are either lost or exist in print but not DVD (seven of them are at Cinematheque Royale de Belgique in Brussels, while one is at EYE in Amsterdam), there are news releases of these films found in trade publications that provide some detail of the type of stunts performed in each movie. For example, in his first big starring role, *Let's Go Gallagher* (*Motion Picture News*, October 1925), Tyler rescued Frankie Darro and his dog from being the direct targets of a train. What can possibly be more exciting in a B-western than Tom Tyler swiftly moving to save a little boy and his dog from imminent destruction perpetrated by the outlaws? *Let's Go Gallagher* put Tom Tyler's first starring role on the Hollywood map, a guarantee of career success which immediately garnered a faithful—if at first youthful—following of matinee goers.

Even more daring stunts would follow in the next handful of Tyler's silent films. In *The Wyoming Wildcat* (1925), Tom leaped off the top of a steep cliff into a rapid whirlpool below to rescue his love object, played by Virginia Southern. He managed to stay afloat of the watery trap, with the girl safely tucked under his strong arms, as he swam to shore and revived her, eventually winning her hand at the end of the story. The "hero rescues a girl from drowning" theme appeared once again in *The Cowboy Musketeer* (1925). Tom rescued his female co-star Frances Dare from drowning in a similar situation, delighting the audience as wide-eyed viewers in awe over the amazing stunts their hero performs in front of them.

In addition to these incredible feats of strength, Tom Tyler was also called on to punch out the bad guys, often taking on more than one or even two at a time when the script requested it. Moving as swiftly as he does, Tom is as agile as he is strong. In *Born to Battle* (1926), Tom took on a whole group of men, putting out their lights rather swiftly, moving like a cat pouncing on a nest of mice. Then in *Red Hot Hoofs* (1926) Tom was a prizefighter who wound up being a cow-puncher on a ranch. He is dressed for the part, and looked the part, with his lean muscular physique, taking on the opponent in the ring.

The one FBO Tom Tyler silent film that exists in DVD format is *The Texas Tornado* (1928). Made the same year he won the AAU Southern California heavyweight weightlifting championship, he once again showcased his athletic prowess. The plot is fairly simple and straightforward: a small family (Jim and Ellen Briscoe with a young adopted son, Buddy Martin) leased a ranch on which the landlord, Latimer, discovers oil on the property, becomes greedy, and wants them off the property so that he can have the oil to himself. Tom Tyler is Tom King, a family relative and financier of the lease but lives in Wyoming. He decides to take a trip to visit the Briscoes, knowing the lease is soon due for renewal and at the same time wants to meet his nephew Buddy for the first time. Buddy is played by Frankie Darro, who would continue to make a total of twenty-six FBO movies with Tom. Watching Tom in action on silent film can produce an adrenalin rush in the engaging viewer: an exciting horseback riding chase where Tom manages to

intercept Latimer by beating him to the bank on time to renew the lease at 3:00 P.M., right before it expires. He changes position on horseback from riding to standing on the saddle, leaping off his horse onto Latimer who is also on horseback, and does so successfully. The climactic scene of Tom rescuing Buddy from a derelict gondola lift dangling in midair from a cable across the canyon is without doubt the best part of "The Texas Tornado." Tom proceeds to climb the cable hand over hand to rescue Buddy, slowly but surely making his way across. He finally arrives at the gondola lift which is about the break as it dangles precariously, Buddy holding onto it for dear life. As soon as the little boy sees Tom edge close to him, Tom encourages him to be brave, wrapping his thin, tiny arms around Tom's strong neck and shoulders as the hero finally makes it back across the cable once again to the safety of the mountain ledge. Buddy is safe, his dog excited to see him, and Tom collapses on the ground, exhausted.

Despite his humble beginnings in Hollywood, Tom Tyler certainly had no problem developing, growing, and maintaining a fan base, which eventually ranged from young boys and girls of his era to B-western and silent film aficionados everywhere. Tom was no ordinary Hollywood actor, to be sure; his shy, reserved demeanor, polite and cooperative manners with everyone, made him highly respected by film makers and co-stars. Tom preferred to spend his spare time working out, gourmet cooking, and cabinetmaking at home. He had more in common with the "guy next door" instead of the biggest names in Hollywood. It is admirable qualities like these and not just his work that make Tom Tyler an actor worth remembering.

Lobby card from 1928's *The Texas Tornado.*

Mary Haberstroh is a Tom Tyler fan and freelance writer. She is also a film researcher and a member of the Scleroderma Foundation.

Drug Use in Silent Cinema:
A Look at the Underbelly of Early Hollywood

by Lewis Walker

Hollywood has become a word that is synonymous with cinema, a place where dreams are realized, stars are born and huge amounts of money are dealt with on a daily basis. It has produced some of the most spectacular things ever to be captured on camera, and produced some of the most recognizable faces of the past century. However, besides the glitz and glamour that has become Hollywood's calling card, there is a dark underside that has ruined careers—and ended lives—for many people in the movie industry. Drugs have played a massive part, both off and on-screen, in shaping the Hollywood that we know today, and some of the most important and drastic changes that have arisen in the past one hundred years has been, in some part, due to the illegal highs.

This article is going to look at the formation of Hollywood as we know it, looking at how prominent drug use was both on the screen and off it. With the formation of Hollywood and the introduction of the actor as a bankable entity, the stars and the characters they played were using drugs more and more, this chapter is therefore going to look at the effect that drugs had on Hollywood until 1920.

Hollywood was chosen as a prime place to shoot films for one simple reason: 355 days of sun out of the year. Films were being shot outside, using natural light and places like New York were not supplying enough. This also gave the film-makers a chance to escape the clutches of the Motion Picture Parent Company, "a syndicate that tried to monopolize the various inventions that had made film-making possible."[1] Famously it was Cecil B. DeMille who was the first to shoot a film in Hollywood in 1913, and before long the center of the film-making industry was placed on the west cost of America—as far away as possible from the regulators in the east. In 1890 the population of California stood at 150,000, but just 25 years later in 1915 this had rocketed to almost one million, which was all due to the migration of the American movie industry.

As Hollywood became more and more successful the studio heads realized that actors could be used to make profit, and that audiences would go to see a film based on who was in it. Until this point actors had been seen as "hired help"[2] but suddenly they were a necessity that could decide whether a film was successful or not. As actors became more and more important to the financial gain of a movie, the money they were paid soared and for many this sudden increase in wealth left them with a lot of disposable income. The first 'star' was an actress called Florence Lawrence who shot to fame after the public were told that she had died. When Lawrence made a public appearance to disprove this fact, Carl Laemmle, a producer, reported that the crowds were so frenzied that they 'tore off her clothes.'[3] Both the fact that she had died and the reaction of the public were false, but the lies meant that Florence Lawrence was now a well known name, and Hollywood's first star earning "$80,000 in 1912."[4] Others soon followed in Lawrence's footsteps, and as the number of recognizable faces increased, as did the salary of each star. This creation of the star

---

[1] David Thomson, *The Whole Equation: A History of Hollywood.* P. 33

[2] Mark Anger, *Hollywood Babylon,* P. 6

[3] Cousins, *The Story of Film,* P. 42

[4] Cousins, *The Story of Film,* P. 42

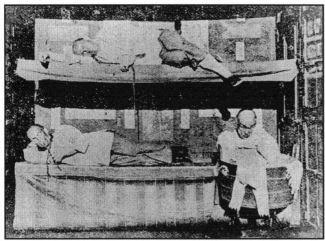

The only surviving still from 1894's *Opium Joint* (Edison).

Cocaine was a relatively new drug in America, it was marketed as a pain killer, being used to aid childbirth and on certain occasions being prescribed to addicts as a cure. It was also an original ingredient in Coca-Cola, which was made from cola nut and coca leaf, "sources of caffeine and Cocaine,"[8] and "by 1906, 80 million Americans were drinking and hoovering up to 11 tons of cocaine a year."[9] The Pure Food and Drug Act was passed in 1906, which meant that all large corporations had to put on the label what was included in the product, and then in 1914 a law was passed that meant that cocaine and other narcotics would be distributed only by doctors orders, and therefore illegal for non-medical use.

system practically happened overnight with certain actors being propelled to stardom, some managed to take "it in their stride; some did not."[5]

While Hollywood was rapidly evolving in the west of America, so was the use of drugs. Around the same time as the invention of cinema, drug use was not seen as a major problem in America and addiction to pain-killers and other prescription drugs carried no stigma. In 1875, nineteen years before Edison debuted his Kinetoscope, San Francisco passed what is considered to be the first law against recreational drug use "banning white people from frequenting opium dens."[6] The first American drug film centers around the use of Opium, being produced in 1894 by W.K. Laurie Dickson for Edison called *Opium Joint*. The plot was basic; "man enters opium den, smokes opium and has weird dreams."[7]

The use of cocaine in Hollywood was widespread, used as cure for tiredness for overworked actors and actresses, and was increasingly used as a source of narrative in the early films. Hollywood was slowly gaining a reputation for excessive use of drugs and alcohol, with many stars "blowing their fortunes on cocaine, unaware of its addictive nature."[10] This image of Hollywood was not helped by the representation of drugs on screen, with a madcap comedy narrative taking prominence in Hollywood involving the uses of drugs. The biggest stars of the time were using drugs as their source of comedy,

---

[5] Kenneth Anger, *Hollywood Babylon*, P. 6

[6] Harry Shapiro, *Shooting Stars: Drugs, Hollywood and the Movies*, P. 17

[7] Jack Stevenson, *Addicted: The Myth and Menace of Drugs in Film*, P. 12

[8] Jack Stevenson, *Addicted: The Myth and Menace of Drugs in Film*, P. 13

[9] Harry Shapiro, *Shooting Stars: Drugs, Hollywood and the Movies*, P. 12

[10] Paul Merton, *Silent Comedy*, P. 171

"THE MYSTERY OF THE LEAPING FISH"

including Charlie Chaplin and Douglas Fairbanks Sr.

Drugs were becoming more of a social problem in America in the early teens with news and scandals splashed across the popular press. The fact that drugs were such a huge part of the public consciousness meant that this was a chance for Hollywood to draw audiences into the cinema's, and thus they started to produce more drug related films. Rather than cashing in on the fears of drugs, Hollywood decided to treat the subject with comedy; "light hearted digs at those funny chinamen and their weird habits or explorations of the funny things people might do under the influence of drugs."[11] Until 1916 many of the drug related films were just a re-telling of the same story, mainly the 1894 film *Opium Joint*, but then Douglas Fairbanks decided to put his own twist on the story of a drug addict.

Douglas Fairbanks began his career as a comedian, making "energetic comedies in which he played young men who personified the optimism of America"[12] but in 1920 a shift to more romantic, heroic leads is what he has become most well known for. Chaplin describes Fairbanks as having "extraordinary magnetism and charm and a genuine boyish enthusiasm which he conveyed to the public."[13] Along with Chaplin, and his second wife, Mary Pickford, Fairbanks is considered as one of the biggest stars of the silent era in Hollywood appealing "to the young" and also "the young at heart."[14] Before Fairbanks's shift to his heroic roles, he made a comedy called *The Mystery of the Leaping Fish* in 1916 which centers around him playing a Sherlock Holmes type of

detective, who, across the two reels, takes a huge amount of cocaine.

In 1916 Fairbanks made 11 films, which made him "a household name"[15] in America, one of which was *The Mystery of the Leaping Fish* where Fairbanks plays the hero, aptly and subtly, named Coke Ennyday. This film is hardly mentioned by biographers of Fairbanks, and by Fairbanks himself, and is overlooked when referring to one of the greatest silent screen stars of Hollywood. The film is directed by John Emerson, supervised by D.W. Griffith, and written by Todd Browning, most famous for directing the horror classics *Dracula* (1931) and *Freaks* (1932). It's amazing, therefore, that a film with so many famous contributors is widely overlooked in the history of cinema, and in the biographies of everyone involved.

The film centers around Coke Ennyday, a detective who tracks down dope dealers in Chinatown to uncover the mystery of the leaping fish, which is a type of flotation device used by holiday makers in the sea. The mystery is that the shop hiring out the leaping fish is a facade for opium dealings, and soon our 'hero' is in the middle of a war on drugs. The slight problem with Coke Ennyday launching a war on drug smuggling is that he is constantly injecting himself with cocaine to gain the necessary energy to carry on with his investigations. The film opens with Coke Ennyday in his office, next to him is a large container labelled 'Cocaine', and behind him the clock face has its numbers replaced with four segments: Dope, Drinks, Sleep and Eats, the hand constantly settles on Dope throughout this first scene to which Ennyday instantly injects himself from his needles handily arranged on his

---

[11] Harry Shapiro, *Shooting Stars: Drugs, Hollywood and the Movies*, P. 24

[12] Jeanine Basinger, *Silent Stars*, P. 99

[13] Charles Chaplin, *My Autobiography*, P. 197-198

[14] Jeanine Basinger, *Silent Stars*, P. 100

[15] Jeanine Basinger, *Silent Stars*, P. 108

"Coke Ennyday, is on our trail!"

belt prepped and ready to use. When watching the film for the first time I was struck by how blatant the drug use was throughout, being described as Basinger as "a bit unsettling today."[16]

I view the film more of a satire on the views on drugs in Hollywood, instead of it championing the use of cocaine. Fairbanks was "somewhat of a health nut, and certainly an early advocate of physical fitness,"[17] and while he was a smoker offscreen there is no mention of him ever taking drugs in a recreational way. In 1916, the year the film was released, many people were starting to question the ethics of Hollywood and the way it was representing drugs on screen.

In 1916 censors were beginning to look towards Hollywood and how its representations of drug use could be controlled. The censors viewed drug use on screen as "powerful, negative, unchecked influences on the impressionable masses,"[18] and wanted to correct this. The start of the First World War meant a sudden decline in the drug comedies that had populated the screens of the early teens, and as more and more soldiers were being treated with anesthetics for their wounds they would return to America with "very real cocaine and opium addictions."[19] In the same year that *The Mystery of the Leaping Fish* was released Aleister Crowley, a British drug expert, commented that Hollywood contained "Cocaine-crazed, sexual lunatics,"[20] painting Hollywood to the public in a very negative light.

With Fairbanks being so health conscience and aware of the accusations made towards Hollywood it is not hard to see this film as a practical joke at the expense of Hollywood, making a laughing-

Jack Pickford and Olive Thomas.

stock of the accusations made towards the industry with the obscene amounts of cocaine that apparently was being used. The use of drugs in the film comes across as quite absurd, and the main source of comedy comes from the amount of drugs that are actually taken onscreen. It's easy to look at the film therefore as a satirical look on how outsiders view Hollywood, and how ridiculous the allegations made against the stars really are. The fact that Coke Ennyday can't even get up out of his chair without three or four injections can be seen as how the public were starting to view the stars at the time of the picture, as people dependent on drugs to achieve the simplest tasks.

[16] Jeanine Basinger, *Silent Stars*, P. 108

[17] Jeanine Basinger, *Silent Stars*, P. 100

[18] Jack Stevenson, *Addicted: The Myth and Menace of Drugs in Film*, P. 15

[19] Jack Stevenson, *Addicted: The Myth and Menace of Drugs in Film*, P. 15

[20] Kenneth Anger, *Hollywood Babylon*, P. 9

No, no, Douglas, you had better give up scenario writing and stick to acting.

The end of the Fairbanks comedies came to end at the same time of a very public scandal hit very close to home for himself and his wife, Mary Pickford. A young starlet named Olive Thomas was married to Jack Pickford, Mary's brother, and was a very successful actress for Selznick Pictures coined by the media as being the 'Ideal American Girl', because she appeared to have the perfect life, and marriage. However at the age of just 20, she was found dead in Paris due to a suspected suicide. The suicide made headlines worldwide, especially seen as she worked for a studio who's slogan was "Selznick Pictures Creates Happy Homes."[21] The investigation into her death discovered that the persona she had on-screen, "a sweet young thing"[22], was very different to her off-screen life. Rumors started to circulate that the reason for her suicide was drug related, which didn't help the view the public had of Hollywood. The story that started to circulate was that Olive Thomas had flown to Paris a few days before her husband, and had been seen out with "some notorious figures of the French underworld; she had sought out some of the roughest, meanest dives of Montmartre."[23] The story went that Olive had tried to obtain a high amount of heroin to supply her husband, who was being labelled as "a hopeless addict"[24], for when he made the trip across. Unable to get the large amounts needed, she had panicked and committed suicide.

Jack Pickford was unable to comment on these allegations because he was under treatment for nervous collapse following Olive's death, but his sister Mary Pickford quickly released a statement "denying such 'sickening aspersions' on her brother's character,"[25] but being involved in a major scandal herself following her divorce and immediate marriage to Douglas Fairbanks meant that this statement was overlooked.

The truth soon followed in a unrelated investigation into a Captain of the United States Army who had sold Cocaine and Heroin in large quantities, keeping names of his clients, one of which was named as the former "Ideal American Girl."[26] The headlines described her as "OLIVE THOMAS, DOPE FIEND"[27] and the truth behind her suicide was suddenly very clear. Basinger's biography of Mary Pickford describes Olive Thomas as a "drug-addict"[28] but makes no mention of Jack Pickford's supposed addictions. Fairbanks's world was suddenly right in the centre of drug related scandals and deaths. The drug related hilarity he had portrayed on screen four years earlier didn't seem that funny anymore, and his career took a turn towards heroic characters instead of drug addicted detectives.

Whether or not the death of Olive Thomas made Fairbanks rethink his career is unclear, but I see it as a big coincidence, especially because it is hardly ever mentioned in works on Fairbanks's career. It could also be down to the fact that the drug comedies of the teens were starting to dwindle by the start of the 1920's, and a more mature, but still uneducated, portrayal of drug use was making its entrance onto the screens of America

---

[21] Kenneth Anger, *Hollywood Babylon*, P. 16

[22] Kenneth Anger, *Hollywood Babylon*, P. 16

[23] Kenneth Anger, *Hollywood Babylon*, P. 16

[24] Kenneth Anger, *Hollywood Babylon*, P. 16

[25] Kenneth Anger, *Hollywood Babylon*, P. 16

[26] Kenneth Anger, *Hollywood Babylon*, P. 18

[27] Kenneth Anger, *Hollywood Babylon*, P. 18

[28] Jeanine Basinger, *Silent Stars*, P. 61

Lewis Walker studied Film Studies at Sheffield Hallam University in England, gaining a Masters degree. He currently live in Dallas having moved to US to get married earlier this year.

Birth of a Nation at 100: Film's Most Influential and Problematic Artifact

by Jeremy Burbick

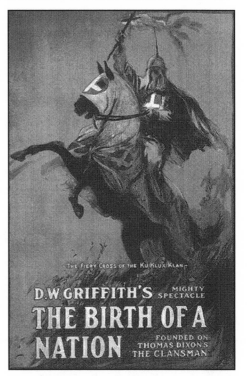

Few films in the history of cinema have had the impact of *Birth of a Nation*. D.W. Griffith's epic, released in early 1915, has arguably been discussed more than any other movie ever made. It's technical merits, cultural impact, overt racism, box-office records, and lasting legacy in Hollywood are all debated to this day.

A century later, scholar Jeremy Burbick provides a 21st century look at the infamous motion picture.

• • •

My first encounter with film's most influential and problematic artifact ended with me unconscious on a couch partly due to boredom. As a teenager in 1995 I bought a used VHS copy of *The Birth of a Nation* for $1.99 from a Blockbuster Video eliminating movies that people no longer rented. I eventually watched the film in its entirety as part of a school project but was unimpressed with the direction and abhorred by the content. This past April, *The Denver Silent Film Festival* marked the 100 year anniversary of *The Birth of a Nation* by screening the picture. Intrigued by the opportunity to watch the film with an audience, I reluctantly I decided to attend.

The Birth of a Nation, which was hailed as a masterwork upon release, announced the arrival of moving pictures as an art form and a legitimate vehicle for storytelling. In the first half of the Twentieth Century, millions of people viewed the film despite protest and censure attempts. *The Birth of a Nation,* based on Thomas Dixon's racist novel *The Clansman,* was a picture by and for white Americans at a time when what we consider racism today was the norm. The film and novel used the example of the Reconstruction Era, 1865-1877, to warn white America of a possible, dire racial problem. Those who saw *The Birth of a Nation* in 1915 thought they received a history lesson.[1] By claiming to use history as its basis, the film tried to legitimize its views. In the hands of Griffith, the power of the medium allowed *The Birth of a Nation* to shape public opinion, to harden long held beliefs, and to convince many whites that the disgraceful way in which black people had been treated, in and out of slavery, was acceptable.[2] The film also glorified and contributed to a resurgence of the nearly forgotten Ku Klux Klan.

---

[1] Melvyn Stokes, *D. W. Griffith's The Birth of a Nation: A History of "The Most Controversial Film of All Time"* (New York: Oxford University Press, 2007), 204

[2] Bruce Chadwick, *The Reel Civil War: Mythmaking in American Film* (New York: Alfred A Knopf, 2001), 14.

By 1914, D. W. Griffith established himself as a top director in the infant American film industry. The distribution length of American films was typically two reels long, around twenty minutes. In comparison, *The Birth of a Nation* ran twelve reels long, over three hours. Actress Lillian Gish relayed the excitement Griffith felt in acquiring Thomas Dixon's novel to adapt to film. "I'm going to use it to tell the truth about the War between the States. It hasn't been told accurately in history books."[3] Griffith, the son of a Confederate Colonel, thought the North misunderstood the South. He also believed the North unwittingly gave the former slaves unwarranted freedoms in the South directly after the war, and the Ku Klux Klan helped restore the social order, paving the way for reconciliation between the States.[4] For his film Griffith envisioned a western, ride-to-the-rescue movie, but "this ride would be to save a nation."[5]

David Wark Griffith in 1919.

Griffith's film premiered in Los Angeles on February 8, 1915 to much acclaim. Griffith slowly released the film to different parts of the country. The protests and attempts at censorship, which followed the film, only added to its allure. The film's debut in Denver occurred on Sunday December 12, 1915 at the Tabor Grand Opera House. Instead of movie houses, Griffith preferred legitimate theaters show his film with an orchestral accompaniment. Screenings ensued twice a day at the Opera House with prices ranging from a quarter to two dollars. According to the *Rocky Mountain News,* those who viewed *The Birth of a Nation* would "be moved until their blood fairly leaps in their veins. It is a series of sights which make civilization ooze up in the human breast."[6] Protests caused Griffith to trim *The Birth of a Nation* and eliminate some of the more offensive scenes. Cuts made to the film included a scene depicting black people being chased through the jungles of Africa, a title card stating that Lincoln's solution to the race problem was to send former slaves to Africa, and shots of black men pulling white women into their cabins in South Carolina.[7] He also added a

Gus's capture by the Klan.

---

[3] Lillian Gish and Ann Pinchot, *The Movies, Mr. Griffith, and Me* (Englewood Cliffs, N. J.: Prentice Hall, 1969), 131.
[4] Ibid, 151, 162.
[5] James Hart, ed., *The Man Who Invented Hollywood: The Autobiography of D. W. Griffith* (Louisville: Touchstone, 1972), 89.
[6] *Rocky Mountain News,* January 2, 1916.
[7] Seymour Stern, "*The Birth of a Nation: 50th* Anniversary," *Film Culture,* Fall 1965, 93.

The Tabor Grand Opera House, circa 1910's.

"There is not a human emotion that is not included somewhere in the story, from the biggest national psychology, to the whim of a petulant girl; from the lowest depths of ruthless villainy, to the utmost grandeur of patriotic ideal."[13]

Over the years, those who defended the film tried to separate Griffith's technical skills and artistry from Dixon's and Griffith's racist propaganda. *Variety* polled two hundred film critics in the 1950's and named *The Birth of a Nation* the greatest motion picture in the first 50 years of the industry.[14] Each decade *Sight and Sound* magazine released a critic and director's poll of the greatest films of all time. In the most recent poll, published in 2012, five critics listed the film as one of the best. The American Film Institute placed the film at 44, in its 1998 list of the "One Hundred Greatest American Movies

disclaimer at the beginning of part two of *The Birth of a Nation* which stated the film should not be viewed as a depiction of any race today.[8] The edits did not lessen the film's racist views.

The Birth of a Nation was a triumphant success. Near the end of the initial run at the Tabor, an ad in the *Denver Post* claimed 80,000 saw the film in Denver in the span of a month.[9] Thomas Dixon acknowledged the value of film by stating, "The moving picture man, author and producer, and exhibitor should take himself more seriously. He is leading a revolution in the development of humanity – as profound a revolution as that which followed the first invention of printing." [10] Griffith's staging, editing, and direction enhanced the appeal of the film. One writer urged her readers to see *The Birth of a Nation*, "for it will make a better American of you".[11] The National Board of Review applauded the film because of its historical accuracy and educational value.[12] *Denver Post* writer Muriel Lee wrote one hundred years ago,

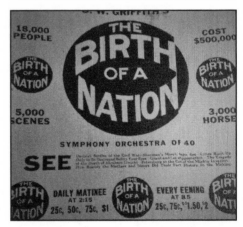

Ads such as these were placed in both *The Rocky Mountain News* and *The Denver Post* during the film's initial release.

[8] *The Birth of a Nation*, shot 621.
[9] *Denver Post*, January 16, 1916.
[10] *Motion Picture News*, July 7, 1923. 46.
[11] Dorothea Dix quoted in Michael Rogan "The Sword Became a Flashing Vision" in Robert Lang, ed. *The Birth of a Nation: D. W. Griffith, Director* (New Brunswick, N. J.: Rutgers University Press, 1994), 277
[12] Ibid.
[13] Muriel Lee, *Denver Post*, December 12, 1915.
[14] Rogan, 250.

Lincoln's assassination remains one of the few scenes that both feels authentic and screens well for today's audiences.

Auditorium. The anniversary provided a legitimate excuse to show the film. The crowd consisted of about one hundred, with the majority being white and middle aged. Only a handful of African Americans and college students attended the screening. Two pianists split musical duty. The Mont Alto Motion Picture Orchestra's Rodney Sauer played part one of the film, while Hank Troy accompanied part two.

Part one of the film focused on two families (one from the North, the other from the South) which intermingled and developed friendships before the outbreak of the Civil War. Members of the two families also became enamored with one another. Love and happiness ended when meddlesome Northern abolitionists inflamed passions, starting the Civil War. After the devastating War which pitted friend against friend, the South lost and Lincoln was assassinated. In the first half of the film, Griffith directed difficult crowd and battle scenes, employed tracking shots, used parallel editing, incorporated color tints to enhance the mood, and edited to build excitement, among other techniques. By comparing *The Birth of a Nation* with the films produced by other film companies circa 1915, Griffith's technical talent and story development exceeded his contemporaries.

For the modern viewer, the second half of the film evoked uneasiness tenfold. According to the film, Radical Republicans' vision for a new South became a nightmare for southerners. Uncontrollable blacks created violence and eroded civilization. In one scene, Griffith depicted the South Carolina State House of Representatives of 1871. Griffith used an impressive technique, where the empty House dissolved in to a chaotic House full of black politicians. After the dissolve, shots

of All Time". In 1980, Anthony Slide claimed, "All those who love cinema will both understand and admire *The Birth of a Nation* for what it is – the ultimate masterpiece of the American silent screen —not what recent detractors have tried to make of it."[15]

The *Birth of a Nation* rarely screened for an audience in the last fifty years. In 2004, successful picketing thwarted an attempted showing of the film at an old Los Angeles film house.[16] The Denver Silent Film Festival recognized the 100 year anniversary of *The Birth of a Nation* by projecting a pristine print of the film in April 2015 at Denver University's Davis

[15] Anthony Slide and Edward Wagenknecht, *Fifty Great American Silent Films, 1912-1920: A Pictorial Survey* (New York: Dover), 20.
[16] Stokes, 277.

depicted black Representatives drinking liquor, taking off their shoes, eating a chicken leg, and celebrating as they passed a law allowing them to marry white women.[17] The scene, and film as a whole, claimed to represent factual occurrences during Reconstruction. However, unlike in the film, black lawmakers showed restraint while legislating during Reconstruction. Black politicians and their political partners, the so-called "carpetbaggers", never held a majority in any southern state, except for a small majority in the lower House of South Carolina. No Reconstruction Congress debated a bill for intermarriage.[18]

Mayhem ensued in *The Birth of a Nation* when black men started to desire and pursue white women. Even the Radical Republican character in the film, Austin Stoneman, recoiled and became angry when his political protégé, the mulatto Lieutenant Governor of South Carolina, asked for his daughter's hand in marriage. Stoneman was based on Thaddeus Stevens, who the film regarded with absolute contempt. When "renegade Negro", Gus, chased after young and pretty Flora Cameron, she jumped to her death while trying to escape from him. Flora's brother, Ben, formed the Ku Klux Klan to enact revenge and reclaim the South for white southerners. The Klan lynched Gus and threw his dead body on the house steps of the Lieutenant Governor, as a warning. Once black people lost their power and were kept in their proper place by intimidation, tranquility returned to the South. Through a racist ideology the North and South reunited and lived happily ever after with the blessing of Jesus Christ, who appears at the end of the film.

African Americans served as extras in *The Birth of a Nation*, but the key characters were played by black faced white actors. The film's unbelievable story and ideology became even more ridiculous when coupled with the images of black faced actors projected on a big screen. White America loved this film one hundred years ago. *The Birth of a Nation* remains one of the largest money making films ever, when adjusted for inflation.[19] The fact the film's story and beliefs play poorly in today's society communicates to how much we have evolved from the racist views of the past.

Denver Silent Film director Howie Movshovitz stated, "*The Birth of a Nation* is important as a cultural artifact that speaks to white America's attitudes towards black America. As a film, it defined extraordinary technical, stylistic, and narrative developments in film, as well as establishing the cinema as a powerful and artistic force."[20] Watching a projected *The Birth of a Nation* allowed me to appreciate Griffith's talent as an innovative director, but his legacy will always be tainted by the beliefs suggested by his film. Griffith helped perpetuate historical myths and racism in this country for decades. *The Birth of a Nation* is a film loathed by Americans today. 100 hundred years ago the film captivated and electrified America, it is important to understand why. Roger Ebert claimed, "If we are to see this film, we must see it all, and deal with it all."[21] And so I have, and now so should you.

Jeremy fell in love with silent film at age 16 and holds a B.A. and an M.A. in history.

---

[17] *The Birth of a Nation*, shots 839-874.
[18] Ira Berliner, ed., *Freedom: A Documentary History of Emancipation, 1861-1867* (NY: Cambridge University Press, 1982) series 2, 733-763.
[19] Stokes, 3.
[20] Interview with Howie Movshovitz, May 15, 2015.
[21] Roger Ebert, *The Great Movies II* (NY: Broadway Books), 66.

Preserving An Piece of Pre-Hollywood Cinema:
The 1907 Chicago Projecting Co.'s Entertainers Supplies Catalog

by Darren Németh

I am the compiler of this 438 page, information packed volume and it supplementary material. It has been two years in the making.

I found this rare catalog back around the late 1980s or early 1990s at an antique shop in Frankenmuth, Michigan while on a trip there with my Grandma. It was on a shelf inside a closet tucked inside a plastic bag with the second edition of *Motion Picture Handbook* by F. H. Richardson from 1912 and possibly another cinema related item. All for a pre-eBay $10. I couldn't believe what had I found and she bought them for me.

I had always been into silent films and movies in general so I recognized the uniqueness of this find. The catalog with its fragile cover has been safe in an archival comic book bag for over twenty five years and handled very carefully the very few times I skimmed through it. The pages are of good crisp, glossy paper but the cover is of thick pulp. The kind that self destructs over the years.

I always thought it would be great to publish this catalog with additional research and other stuff added so others can see it. Thankfully a few seemingly easy to do self publishing opportunities popped up over the past several years on the internet. However, in order get this in print the binding would have to be be disassembled, ruining any value it would have both as an artifact and as a book. This was the only way to scan it properly. Since the cover was in delicate shape I figured it was best to wait until it fell off. I would not feel as bad ruining it that way. Then around mid to late 2012 the front cover separated off from what was left of the spine and that gave me the go ahead to carefully take the book apart.

The binding was made up of multiple combined leafs fastened together with two thick steel staples. The cover pasted on at the spine. The staples were taken out allowing me to lay the individual pages evenly flat on the scanner. All were scanned at 600 dpi in color with no corrective effects applied. This took about 8 hours. I

Complete Optigraph Motion Picture Machine, Model 1907

spent an additional 80 hours gently retouching each of its over 330 pages. In 2014 I spent the winter in my heated sun room and at the public library doing research and compiling the 23 page, double-column index.

The Chicago Projecting Company was one of the major players in early cinema but totally forgotten today. They were dealers in all items that someone needed to be in the exhibition end of the motion picture business from around 1899 to 1913.

Their catalog and merchandise was available through mail order, much like a Sears and Roebuck catalog. Hopeful entrepreneurs would see their ads in working class magazines like the *Saturday Evening Post*, *Popular Mechanics* and *Colliers* promising a profitable and easy to run business.

I included the majority of the Chicago Projecting Co.'s ad layouts they placed in magazines from 1899 to 1913.

The start up costs for getting into the business however were enormous and by 1907 the traveling movie showman business as the main mode people saw films was on its way out. Vaudeville troops and nickel admission movie theaters (nickelodeons) whose films were supplied by film exchanges were gaining popularity. And the fact that the traveling showman had to buy his own prints and slides outright limited what he would show. They were also exorbitantly expensive and easily damaged while out on the road.

Catalog No. 122 is extremely rare as well as everything else from the era. Similar movie business items of a much later vintage are more common because they were stashed away in theater offices and closets, forgotten until decades later. However, when this catalog was published at the turn of the century independent traveling showman went from town to town on a train or by wagon and discarded things that had no use to them. Much like when films and slide sets no longer had commercial value. One less thing to lug around and keep track of.

Rutgers University has Catalog No. 120, No. 123 from 1907,

CHICAGO PROJECTING CO.,
Motion Picture Exhibition Tents.

and 126 from 1908 on microfilm. An additional archive has another and as of this writing there is a No. 121 that has been on eBay for seemingly forever. Another collector in Germany has a later one from 1909.

I am probably the only person willing to destroy one of them and its great value in order to scan the pages, correct the out of sequence page numbering and index it all.

Until now the Rutgers microfilm is the only one available to the public to view and it not easy to get access to.

In this deluxe reprint you will find a considerable amount of information about what was needed to get into the optical business and a feel of what it was like for the average person to be in it and also what the environment was like to see a movie in 1907. This is all Pre-Hollywood. Before movie theaters sprung up in every town in the USA. The era of one angle shot, one minute films, stage bound tableaux, and Méliès trick films.

The longest acted out films listed in the catalog are *Kit Carson* (1903, American Mutoscope & Biograph) at 1,184 feet and *The Impossible Voyage* (1904, Star-Film) at 1,075 feet. Both lasting a little more than ten minutes. The 5,575 foot *Jeffries-Sharkey Contest*, a famous boxing event in Coney Island from 1899, is the longest actuality at around 135 min. The majority of the rest of the more than 1,000 films sold in this catalog are under sixty to ninety seconds in duration.

The average traveling show usually, but not always, had a magic lantern slide show and 10-20 minutes of film. Music was supplied by either someone part of the traveling group, local talent or a talking machine.

An "advance man" was in the next town setting up promotion for the next event. Advertising was through handouts and posters and sometimes the local news paper.

Over 1,000 motion pictures, 1,000 magic lantern slides and sets are in this catalog. These are all fully indexed in the back, as well as over 250 pieces of Graphophone talking machine, Optigraph, stereopticon, and other items essential to operate in the trade that were offered COD through your local express office.

Pre-Hollywood cinema is rarely written about because so little documentation from that era survives today. Many distributors, manufactures and businesses came and went and the independent showman threw their gear out to find other work once theaters made the trade obsolete.

Scholars and early cinema fans will surely find some value in the 438 pages of my deluxe reprint of the *1907 Chicago Projecting Co.'s Entertainer's Supplies Catalog No. 122: Deluxe Edition*.

For more information and to order the catalog, visit: www.giantsquidaudiolab.com/1907/ catalog.html

Drama Treatment Enters Comedy Photography:
Comedy Cinematographer of Features Must Know Dramatic Value in Work

by Walter Lundin, A.S.C.
Chief Cinematographer,
Harold Lloyd Productions

Much of the focus of *Silent Film Quarterly* is on the actors and actresses of the silent era, as well as (to a lesser extent) early directors. For this issue's classic article, however, we felt it was important to highlight a man who spent his entire career behind the camera filming some of the most beloved films in cinematic history. Walter Lundin, pictured below manning the camera for 1929's *Welcome Danger*. Lundin was Lloyd's longtime cinematographer, dating back to the "Lonesome Luke" days and continuing to work with Harold until *The Cat's Paw*.

During his tenure with Harold Lloyd Productions, Lundin worked on such masterpieces as *Safety Last, Haunted Spooks, Hot Water, Girl Shy, The Freshman, The Kid Brother, Speedy,* and *For Heaven's Sake*. It was at the peak of his prowess that he wrote the following article for the June, 1924 issue of the *American Cinematographer*. It is important to remember the lesser-known men and women who played critical, if not visible, roles in the development of Hollywood. Walter Lundin certainly ranks amongst the most talented of these unsung heroes.

• • •

Those pioneers who began to observe cinematographic tendencies several years ago were of the unanimous opinion that being a "comedy cameraman" meant an

ability to do "trick stuff" and to turn out hard, wire-sharp, black-and-white negative.

At the time they made their observations they were right. But comedies, like other phases of film production, have progressed, and cinematography in comedies has likewise risen to a different plane.

Story Subordinate

In the olden days, comedies, I might say, were objective to an extremity. All action, never a dull moment, keep the audience on the edge of the chair, story and plot always subordinate to gags.

Comedies must still have their gags, but even therewith, this medium of motion picture entertainment is no longer identified with action at any cost—and there is still plenty of action—but has, on the contrary I might again hazard an opinion, begun to stroll on paths of the subjective. By that I mean that comedies of the outstanding class are no longer a series of incoherent situations which, though laughable, were not always quite reasonable.

Story Carried Throughout

No, the feature-length comedy has changed this. There is a thread of story that runs through the channel of humor; there are drama and moments of pathos in the most hilarious of comedies—and all this directly affects the cinematographer who films such productions.

Doomed to Obscurity

How often in the old days did the comedy cinematographer look at the work of his fellow artist, the dramatic cinematographer, as it was flashed on the screen, rich in atmospheric effects, and wish that he would have the opportunity of essaying something as pretentious. But unless he would leap to the ranks of the dramatic, he could do little more than wish. Instead, he would go to the studio the next day and find consolation in photographing some particularly

hazardous piece of action or in creating some new trick—which, mind you, are not for a moment to be belittled.

Public's Tastes

But the majority of that small minority of motion picture patrons who have ever recognized photography in the least, always have been impressed with something "beautiful"—such as lovers under the blossoming trees in springtime, etc., etc. They may have a faint idea that comedy cinematography entails danger to life and limb as well as a knowledge of the most intricate details of the camera, but even with this suspicion they are never able to place it on a plane of comparison with the dramatic.

The feature-length comedy, however, with its plot, its recognition of the subjective as well as the objective, its points of pathos and drama, has changed the outlook of the cinematographer making the same. He is no longer consigned to the oblivion of what is considered as ordinary, but is given the opportunity to step forth with sequences, the photography in which vies with that in dramas for pictorial beauty that arrests the attention of the critically inclined.

Atmospheric Treatment

Those dramatic moments, which have been injected into the feature comedy to attract sympathy to the star for instance, may be treated atmospherically—which is just what the comedy cinematographer has been waiting for, for years. He can play for effects that will appeal to those who are impressed with the pictorially beautiful. By his photography he can show that he has a sense of dramatic values as well as of comedy situations.

Versatility Required

All of which calls for the utmost versatility on the part of the comedy cinematographer. Not only must he be able to "turn his camera inside out" for trick stuff as has so aptly been said, not only must he have the nerves of an iron man, but he must be able to make his work compare with that of the most favorable of his fellow artists who have made their reputations in dramatic motion pictures.

Without committing myself to appraising cinematography in Harold Lloyd productions, I may safely say that it was our endeavor at least to imbue certain sequences of recent Lloyd productions with atmospheric dramatic treatment. I refer in particular to "Dr. Jack," "Grandma's Boy," "Safety Last," and "Girl Shy." If the reader who viewed these productions recalls, it will be remembered that there were not a few scenes in them that were far removed from old-school comedy. They truly were gems of drama and pathos.

Dramatic Cinematography

What did this mean for the cinematographer? Should he film such scenes very "contrasty" with plenty of "black and white" as he would do in straight comedy episodes? Or was it his duty to give the sequence the treatment it deserved—and that treatment of course would be dramatic treatment. Clearly there was only one logical thing to be done—leave the beaten path of comedy cinematography and make the camera lens see drama. And that is what we tried to do in shot after shot.

But no matter how much drama he must have in his stock of wares the comedy cinematographer is, after all, essentially a trickster, and there is scarcely a comedy that passes that he is not called upon to run the gamut of camera intricacies. And never does he escape the element of personal danger. Whenever a member of the cast takes his life into his hands, then the cinematographer, you may be assured whether the audience realizes it or not, is

taking a similar chance. Every comedy cinematographer knows this and can prove it by his own experiences. I personally can bear testimony to the statement by virtue of the seven years I have spent with Harold Lloyd—and who can count the narrow escapes that this star has had in his comedies in that time!

"Safety Last" of course was one succession of perils, and you can be assured that the cinematographer was immediately present in all of the perils.

Throughout the entire shooting of the thrill action in "Safety Last," there was an element of danger not only for Lloyd but for the cinematographer. In the scenes showing Lloyd as a "human fly," climbing up the side of a building, the Bank of Italy Building, Los Angeles, was used. This building is twelve stories high. In order to shoot down on Lloyd as he was ascending, it was necessary to erect a platform that projected out over the street. It extended something like ten feet beyond the building limit, and you can believe me, it was quite a sensation following the climb from that heighth.

Although in seven years with Lloyd, we have escaped with nothing more than minor injuries, we believe it is only because the fates have been kind to us. We had a very narrow call in shooting some of the scenes in "Girl Shy" when Lloyd drove a team of lightning fast horses down the main streets of Los Angeles. One of out shots showed the galloping horses flying clean over the camera. We mounted the camera in a manhole on Grand Avenue. Several times the scene was made but not perfectly. The last time we attempted it, one of the horses swerved just a little as it approached the manhole, and it was only by the merest of chance that the camera and its manipulator escaped collision with flying hoofs.

Silent Soaps:
A Unique Homage to the
Silent Era

It was when I was visiting the Niles Essanay Silent Film Museum that I first became aware of Silent Soaps. The novelty of such a product struck me as remarkable —who would think to combine their love of soap making with an appreciation of early cinema? It is also important to mention that the scents were all wonderful and the packaging beautifully executed. *Silent Film Quarterly* was able to reach out to Chris Whittman of Cats in the Cradle Soap, the brand responsible for the Silent Soaps line. Chris described the process behind making such unique soaps and the men and women who influence the line of products most. If you're looking for a unique gift for the silent film-lover in your life, or just want to support an independent soap maker paying tribute to the early days of cinema, look no further than Silent Soaps.

• • •

Can you describe how you decided to start making such a unique product as silent film-inspired soap?

As a soap maker I wanted to do something to generate interest in the great silent film comedians so it seemed natural to put the images of my favorite ones on the wrappers of particular soaps, and in so doing try to keep the scents and formulas in keeping with what might have been popular in the silent film era. Buster

Keaton was my first, and it seemed fitting to give him my most popular soap, Bay Rum.

For those of us who are unacquainted with the process, how do you go about designing a new type of soap?

I choose scents that are personal favorites and incorporate skin moisturizing and soothing natural ingredients. With the exception of a few soaps I make, base oils are fairly uniform for all soaps.

How did you select the silent film stars you based soaps on?

My husband and I have our favorites, and we've been collecting their films for quite a few years now. Keaton was the first silent film comedian to capture our hearts and he was the first to grace a bar of soap. We also enjoy the films of many others and some of them are now on my soap wrappers. Originally I chose 5 silent film comedians and then added Thelma Todd as the 6th at the bequest of a film historian who is particularly fond of Thelma's films. Apparently Thelma's favorite flower was the violet. I made a fabulous violet soap but now I can no longer obtain the same fragrance oil. I will probably go with a rose or other floral scent for Thelma's bar in future.

Have you gotten much response from the silent film community?

Unfortunately there is a limited audience for the Silent Soaps. Many people still do not know much about silent film

comedians or silent films, particularly the younger generation. It's been disappointing but I persevere. I thought a few of the museums or vintage theatres would like to carry them but few have. There are really nice photos and short bios with each bar, on the outside wrappers as well as inside and that helps give a bit of insight into each comedian.

Lastly, if you could add any actor or actress to your line of products who would it be?

That's easy! I would love to add Laurel & Hardy, but copyright issues, licensing fees, etc. would make it far too expensive. Most folks don't even know that Laurel and Hardy did many wonderful silent films in addition to their talkies, both individually and paired as a team. We own a lot of them, and they never fail to bring a laugh no matter how many times we watch them.

For more information about Silent Soaps and to order your own bar, visit:
www.catsinthecradlesoap.com

Several of the silent-themed soaps that Cats in the Cradle offers. The company celebrates a time when "Comedy was King....and the Movies were Clean!"

The Forgotten Actress Series: A Foray into Silent Film Fiction

I first ran into Laini Giles at Cinecon 51 in September of 2015. We were both perusing the festival's extensive memorabilia sale, and I overheard her mention to someone her recent novel on silent film actress Olive Thomas. I was very familiar with *The Forgotten Flapper*, having seen numerous reviews online, so I introduced myself and my publication (which had only one issue released at the time).

The next week I paid Laini Giles a phone call to discuss her first novel, which I had read in the interim. Thoroughly impressed by the attention to detail about a fairly obscure actress, I was excited to hear what sparked her to write such a book. "I love historical fiction of any kind," she explained, "especially when it takes place between 1900 and 1930. I read a book a few years ago called *Loving Frank* [by Nancy Horan] about Frank Lloyd Wright's mistress. It was amazing, so vivid, and I thought, 'That's what I want to do.' I love the blending of fact with fiction."

The rise and fall of Olive Thomas certainly lends itself to retelling, and for Laini, the choice of actress was easy. "Olive Thomas was a natural first subject for me, because she lived this beautiful topsy-turvy life."

Topsy-turvy it certainly was. Obviously the most controversial aspect of her young life was her mysterious death France in 1920. Although conspiracy theories abound, Giles chose the simplest possibility —"I picked what made the most sense to me," she stated simply. "Murder seemed crazy. Jack [Pickford] was spoiled rich, but he wasn't a bad guy. An accidental overdose seemed like the most likely scenario to me."

The success of *The Forgotten Flapper* inspired Giles to quickly start thinking about another book in the same series. "I quickly realized that it doesn't have to be one book, so I thought, 'Who else can I do?'" Clara Bow is next in the "Forgotten Actress Series," but beyond that she's keeping her subjects secret. "There were plenty of hard-luck gals during the silent and early sound periods" who she plans on paying homage too, and she already has her next five or six books lined up.

Fortunately, more films starring Clara Bow survive than those with Olive Thomas. "*The Forgotten Flapper* was almost all book research, with little access to her movies," Giles lamented, although she did note 1920's *The Flapper* (with Thomas in the title role) as a favorite. Miss Bow will certainly give her more material to work from.

Laini Giles concluded our chat by talking about the support she has received from silent film fans worldwide. "The book has had an amazing response," she proudly explained, "and I've been overwhelmed with support. It began in silent film Facebook groups. Martin Turnbull, author of the Garden of Allah novels, helped show me the way to go. Since the book came out I've attended Cinecon [in Los Angeles] and had readings and signings in Calgary and Vancouver."

The "Forgotten Actress Series" is certainly a noble endeavor and one which Silent Film Quarterly supports fully. Stay tuned in future issues for news regarding Laini Giles's novelization of the life of Clara Bow, as well as her additional books.

For more information and to order The Forgotten Flapper, *visit:*
www.lainigiles.com

Manufactured by Amazon.ca
Bolton, ON

35175027R00037